Church as Dynamic Life-System

Catholicity in an Evolving Universe
Ilia Delio, General Editor

This series of original works by leading Catholic figures explores all facets of life through the lens of catholicity: a sense of dynamic wholeness and a conscious awareness of a continually unfolding creation.

CATHOLICITY IN AN EVOLVING UNIVERSE

Church as Dynamic Life-System

*Shared Ministries and
Common Responsibilities*

JOSEPH A. BRACKEN, SJ

ORBIS BOOKS
Maryknoll, New York 10545

Founded in 1970, Orbis Books endeavors to publish works that enlighten the mind, nourish the spirit, and challenge the conscience. The publishing arm of the Maryknoll Fathers and Brothers, Orbis seeks to explore the global dimensions of the Christian faith and mission, to invite dialogue with diverse cultures and religious traditions, and to serve the cause of reconciliation and peace. The books published reflect the views of their authors and do not represent the official position of the Maryknoll Society. To learn more about Maryknoll and Orbis Books, please visit our website at www.maryknollsociety.org.

Library of Congress Cataloging-in-Publication Data

Names: Bracken, Joseph A., author.
Title: Church as dynamic life-system : shared ministries and common responsibilities / Joseph A. Bracken.
Description: Maryknoll : Orbis Books, 2019. | Series: Catholicity in an evolving universe | Includes bibliographical references and index.
Identifiers: LCCN 2018041124 (print) | LCCN 2018055223 (ebook)| ISBN 9781608337774 (e-book) | ISBN 9781626983151 (pbk.)
Subjects: LCSH: Church. | Catholic Church—Doctrines. | Teilhard de Chardin, Pierre. | Whitehead, Alfred North, 1861–1947.
Classification: LCC BX1746 (ebook) | LCC BX1746 .B68 2019 (print) | DDC 262—dc23
LC record available at https://lccn.loc.gov/2018041124

*This book is fondly dedicated
to the people of St. Columban Parish
in Loveland, Ohio,
from whom I learned what it means
to be a participant in a dynamic life-system.*

Contents

Acknowledgments

At an age of life when people take care of their health and in some cases start writing their personal memoirs, I was encouraged by an academic colleague and good friend, Ilia Delio, to undertake a major project, namely, to use the systems-oriented approach to reality that I have developed over the years to write a book about the church as an evolving corporate life-system as well as the stable institutional entity that has existed basically unchanged for two thousand years. Such a project would be in line with the spirit of the *Pastoral Constitution on the Church in the Modern World (Gaudium et spes)* at the Second Vatican Council and might reawaken enthusiasm for the sharing of ministries and responsibilities at the parish level, especially among the non-ordained members of the parish. Fortunately, Ilia Delio was in a position—as an editor for a series on catholicity, published by Orbis Books—to turn possibility into reality. She recommended the idea to Robert Ellsberg, the publisher of Orbis Books, and he in turn arranged for me to get a contract and start to work on the manuscript. So to both Ilia Delio and Robert Ellsberg I owe special thanks for shaking me out of my reveries about the past and doing something more constructive at this time of my life.

Systems-oriented thinking has already appeared, of course, in a few of my previous book publications: *Subjectivity, Objectivity, and Intersubjectivity: A New Paradigm for Religion and Science* (Templeton Foundation Press, 2009); *Does God Roll Dice? Divine Providence for a World in the Making* (Liturgical Press, 2012); and *The World in the Trinity: Open-Ended Systems in Science and Religion* (Fortress Press, 2014). I used insights contained in these three books in thinking through and eventually formulating the first three chapters of the present book. So to the editors and publishers of these three academic presses I owe a long-term debt of thanks for helping me develop my thoughts over the years in terms of systems-oriented thinking. The same thanks naturally could be extended to the editors of academic journals like *Theology and Science, Zygon, American Journal of Philosophy and Theology, Horizons,* and *Theological Studies* insofar as they too provided space for my reflections, first on the topic of *field* and then on the topic of *system* as foundational metaphor in a new process-oriented metaphysics. Finally, I make multiple references and in some cases relatively brief citations to the works of many other authors, living and dead. To one and all, a debt of thanks for the material help that they thereby directly or indirectly provided for this book. As someone who strongly believes in our human interdependence for everything we think, say, and do, I could do no less in penning a word of thanks to all those who in their own way contributed to the composition of this book.

Foreword

Ilia Delio

In 2015 Pope Francis issued the encyclical *Laudato si': On Care for Our Common Home*, calling attention to the problem of global warming. The radical nature of the encyclical lay in its attention to the concrete problems of the environment and the growing gap between rich and poor. By challenging both church and world to move from individualism and consumerism to interdependency, the pope indicated that our worldview must change if we are to anticipate a sustainable future.

In this new book Joseph Bracken builds on the need for an interdependent framework by focusing on the church as a dynamic life-system. He offers a significantly new concept of church that shifts our attention from a static, fixed structure to one that participates in the overarching cosmic life-system that sustains all life on earth. Bracken's aim is to highlight the collective responsibility of all individual church members and of the church itself as a collective reality in order to raise conscious responsibility for preserving the environment. This is not only a noble aim but a much needed one, as the reality of global warming threatens the very survival of humankind.

There is no doubt that the church struggles to navigate a path through the uncharted process of evolution; however, I could not think of a better person to write a book dealing with the church, evolution, and the environment than Joseph Bracken. A philosopher by training and a disciple of Alfred

North Whitehead, Bracken has uniquely forged a paradigm of dynamic life-systems to address the evolution of life both philosophically and theologically. He does not make sweeping claims or conflate medieval philosophy and modern science; rather, he carefully and explicitly constructs his system of thought from the ground up, that is, by providing a reasonable philosophical basis to his ideas enabling him to articulate a new understanding of God and world. In formulating his ideas, he goes beyond Whitehead's system of individualized atoms by positing the notion of the system as a fundamental starting point, a conceptual position that is consistent with modern science. A system is a set of interrelated elements that make a unified whole. Even individual entities—like plants, people, schools, or economies—are themselves systems and at the same time cannot be fully understood apart from the larger systems in which they exist. A systems approach helps people understand the complexity of the world around them and encourages them to think in terms of relationships, connectedness, and context. Naturalist John Muir writes: "When we try to pick out anything by itself, we find it hitched to everything else in the universe."

Whereas Western science, especially after Galileo, focused on things that can be measured and quantified, systems thinking posits that relationships among individual parts may be more important than the parts themselves. An ecosystem, for example, is not just a collection of species but includes living things interacting with one another and their nonliving environment. In the systems view the "objects" of study are networks of relationships. Bracken grounds his systems approach in a philosophical framework of creativity that undergirds not only the self-constitution of actual entities but the formation of societies. It is the interacting components of a society that give rise to collective creativity, which in turn affects a socially organized world. The theological ground of collective creativity is the Trinity, which Bracken describes as a "divine Life-system that includes within its all-encompassing field of activity all the finite life-systems making up the world in which we live." By drawing panentheistic connections between the Trinity as creative society and the church as creative society, Father Bracken is able to envision the church as a dynamic life-system and thus part of the larger community of life-giving systems. In this respect he offers a new understanding of ministry in the church and the role of the church in relation to the world. Rather than focusing on individual ministries or persons, he highlights the interaction between the common or shared field of activity among ministries, the dynamic system of church, and the larger world systems. His is a paradigm of interdependency and cooperativity. Human reality is grounded in the ongoing existence of communities more than in the transient existence and activity of individual human beings who make up those communities. In this respect communities are not extrinsic to persons; rather community is the basis of personhood.

This is an exciting book because it regards the church not as an institution composed of rules and laws but a life-system of interacting entities, in whom creativity becomes its defining power and purpose. Although creativity as a philosophical concept is grounded in the eternal movement from potentiality to actuality, the concept of emerging life as creative life is consonant with the message of Jesus of Nazareth. Gospel life is about the dynamism of relationships, the formation of community and emerging wholeness grounded in the Life-system of the Trinity.

Once you read this book, you will think about the church and Christian life in a new way. Bracken offers a new structural paradigm that moves us beyond fixity and substance to relationality and movement. Only if we begin to think in terms of relationality and community can we move toward a sustainable ecology of life. As Pope Francis indicates, the turn toward an ecological system of life is not an option; it is an imperative. Father Bracken makes a significant contribution to the pope's vision by offering a new structure of dynamic systems. God is not simply Creator; rather, God is the eternal dynamic Life-system of endless creativity: "See, I am making all things new!"

Church as Stable Institution and as Evolving Life-System

What is the church? Is it a religiously ordered institution with headquarters (at least for Roman Catholics) in Rome, or is it a group of people who attend mass at the same local church every weekend? Or is it both an established institution and a particular local congregation at the same time, although in different ways? In St. Paul's First Epistle to the Corinthians, the church is described as the body of Christ (1 Cor 12:13); in the Epistle to the Ephesians, the church is the Temple of God with Christ Jesus as the capstone (Eph 2:19–22); finally, in the Epistle to the Hebrews, it is the New Jerusalem (Heb 12:22–24). Of these three expressions, the one that I favor is the church as the body of Christ in First Corinthians, for a physical body is an organic unity in diversity of parts or members in ongoing dynamic relation to one another. I, for example, am the ongoing byproduct or result of the interaction of my mind and body, and within my body the ongoing interaction of heart, lungs, nerves, muscles, skin, and so on. In that sense I am a functioning life-system as much as, or even more than, myself as (in the conventional sense) a member of the human race.

Furthermore, I am a growing life-system, not an unchanging machine. As a life-system I am always changing or evolving in my customary way of thinking or acting in response to other human beings and the world around me. A machine, on the contrary, works best if it never changes in its customary mode of operation. It is designed to function in basically the same way wherever it is located in space, and at night just as well as during the day. Thus, it is a nonliving, deterministic system with inanimate parts or members. All the living things of this world are, on the contrary, evolving or open-ended systems with parts or members that are alive, actively engaged with other parts or members of the system.

Applying this distinction between open-ended and closed systems to the church as the body of Christ, I propose that the church works best if it functions as an open-ended system in ongoing exchange with other systems or corporate entities (both religious and secular) that are likewise open-ended in their relations with one another. The church, however, suffers or at least declines in vitality if it functions as a relatively closed system with little positive exchange with other systems or corporately organized entities in its environment. Cooperation among systems for the sake of some commonly agreed upon goals and values sets up a favorable social environment for the continued existence and activity of all the systems that in one way or another are involved. On the contrary, jealous competition among systems for achievement of individual and narrowly conceived goals and values tends to create a hostile environment unfavorable to the continued survival and prosperity of all the systems thereby involved. Hence, it is in the long-term interest of the church to cooperate with other life-sustaining systems in maintaining an environment in which all can thrive and grow.

Yet, in thus claiming that the church is (or at least should be) an open-ended rather than a closed life-system, I do not exclude the equally important reality of the church as a stable institutional entity, for the church even as an open-ended system is historically grounded. That is, it always embodies in its current structure and mode of operation its past history up to the present moment. Yet at every moment in that long historical process of growth and development, the church has a formal structure and ongoing mode of operation. Otherwise, it would never exist as anything definite to which one can give one's loyalty. Admittedly, this non-dual reality of the church as both ongoing historical process and determinate institutional entity from moment to moment can result in tension, if not open conflict, among members of the church. Some Christians focus so much on the church as a determinate entity here and now that they lose sight of the multiple changes in church structure and mode of operation that have taken place even in their own lifetime. Others, however, are so fascinated with the notion of the church as in constant need of reform and renewal that they become much too impatient with the inevitably slow pace of change within the church, given its reality as a complex worldwide organization. Yet sustained dialogue between these rival interest groups within the church should lead to a compromise position on the nature of the church that is aware of its successes and failures in the past and at the same time open to whatever challenges the future might bring.

In advance of setting forth in detail my understanding of the church as an open-ended system, however, I first review in Chapter 1 and Chapter 2 the efforts of two earlier philosopher/theologians to come to terms with the implications of an organic or systems-oriented approach to physical reality in general and to the Christian-God-world relationship in particular. The authors that I have in mind are Pierre Teilhard de Chardin, a French Jesuit priest doing pioneering work in archeology and paleontology before World War II, and Alfred North Whitehead, a distinguished British mathematician and theoretical physicist, who together with Bertrand Russell wrote the influential book *Principia Mathematica* and developed a theory of relativity comparable to that of Albert Einstein. Teilhard, in *The Phenomenon of Man* (later retitled *The Human Phenomenon*) and other works, set forth his personal vision of a Christian understanding of cosmic evolution. This vision would be grounded in a slow process of trial and error and yet, ultimately, culminate in a divinely predetermined Omega Point—the mystical body of Christ as envisioned in the opening chapter of the Pauline epistles to the Ephesians and Colossians

(Eph 1:7–10; Col 1:15–20). Alfred North Whitehead likewise challenged the conventional understanding of evolution in the natural world with his claim that the ultimate units of physical reality are not inert bits of matter (for example, atoms and molecules) controlled in their ongoing interaction by external forces like gravity, but instead mini-organisms, that is, corporate unities of interrelated parts or members (for example, atoms and molecules) with an internal principle of self-organization so as to evolve and grow in size and complexity of organization. Thus, both Teilhard and Whitehead reintroduced purposiveness, meaning, and value (the distinguishing marks of a life-system) into the scientific understanding of the cosmic process—a process that was otherwise considered to be largely deterministic, equivalent to the workings of a cosmic machine. Yet each of them proceeded from a different perspective in writing his cosmology: Whitehead as more philosopher of science than theologian; Teilhard de Chardin as more theologian than philosopher of science.

In Chapter 3 I set forth my synthesis of the thought of Teilhard de Chardin and Alfred North Whitehead in terms of a trinitarian systems-oriented approach to reality. That is, I contend that the three divine Persons in and through their ongoing interaction co-constitute a divine Life-system that includes within its all-encompassing field of activity or mode of operation all the finite life-systems making up the world in which we live. Hence, this systems-oriented understanding of the Christian God-world relationship is a type of panentheism in which the world of creation exists within God and yet maintains an independence from God in its own finite mode of operation. For, as I see it, only with this antecedent philosophical understanding of reality can I logically set forth in Chapter 4 my particular understanding of the church as a historically grounded life-system within a world constituted by life-systems that are sometimes aligned with one another and yet at other times in competition with one another.

I concede that, for most of the church's long history, priority has been given to the church as an authoritative institutional entity rather than to the way in which all members of the church in various ways have a voice in spreading the message of the gospel. Yet, in the current atmosphere of the post–Vatican II Catholic Church, priority seems to be shifting to the church as an organic reality, a life-system that requires much more active participation in church life on the part of all its members in order to function well. In particular, the classical top-down relationship of clergy and laity within the church, in which the laity are only expected to be obedient to the teachings of the church as prescribed by the church's magisterium, is currently being challenged by a new understanding of ministry within the church. All church members are ministers of the gospel message by reason of their baptism. Only some church members are chosen for the special kind of ministry that involves administration of the sacraments and for ongoing church governance in virtue of the sacrament of holy orders.

In Chapter 5, I suggest that the church as a dynamic life-system should be seen as likewise participant in the overarching cosmic life-system that sustains all life on this earth. What I have in mind here is the collective responsibility of all church members—both individually and collectively—to take conscious responsibility for preserving the environment. Here I have recourse in the first place to Pope Francis's encyclical *Laudato si'* with its emphasis on taking care of our common home. In my judgment, Pope Francis is implicitly thinking here in terms of a systems-oriented or process-oriented approach to physical reality and, in particular, vis-à-vis the environment. But, writing from a pastoral rather than an explicitly philosophical perspective, he does not make clear (or perhaps is not even aware) that he has moved out of the context of classical metaphysics with its emphasis on individual entities (substances) into a more socially organized, systems-based approach to reality with its emphasis on common human responsibility for preservation of the environment. Accordingly, in Chapter 5 I also offer some comments on the work of an eminent environmentalist, Holmes Rolston III, in his books *Environmental Ethics* (1998) and *A New Environmental Ethics*

(2012). Rolston is obviously more at home in a systems-oriented approach to reality than Pope Francis is in *Laudato si'*.

Finally, in a brief epilogue I recount how, over time, I came to embrace a systems-oriented approach to reality and thus to lay the foundation for an understanding of church as a dynamic life-system as well as an enduring institutional entity.

Chapter 1

Teilhard's Theological Vision

Pierre Teilhard de Chardin, Roman Catholic priest and natural scientist specializing in geology and paleontology (the study of fossils), was born in Auvergne, France, in 1881. His mother was a devout Catholic with a special love for the Christian mystical tradition and, above all, devotion to the Sacred Heart of Jesus. His father was a professional archivist with a keen interest in geology that he shared with his children on walks in the countryside around their house, which was pockmarked by ancient volcanic eruptions. Hence, from his parents Teilhard inherited both a love of the natural world as a fascinating evolutionary process and a thirst for an all-embracing mystical vision of the meaning and value of cosmic history and human life in terms of God's ongoing presence and activity in the natural world. Both of these aspirations found expression in Teilhard's literary career, above all, in his master work, *The Human Phenomenon,* which was started in the late 1920s but only published posthumously in 1955.[1] Teilhard's caution in providing for the publication of this book only after his death was presumably due to his fear of censure by the teaching authority of the Catholic Church and concern that he would not receive approval for publication of the book by his Jesuit

---

[1] Pierre Teilhard de Chardin, *The Human Phenomenon*, trans. Sarah Appleton-Weber (Brighton, OR: Sussex Academic Press, 1999).

7

superiors in France. He also anticipated the critique of more secular-minded natural scientists, above all, those scientists interested in cosmology and the origin of life on this earth from a purely naturalistic perspective. Yet Teilhard was convinced that the natural order and the realm of the supernatural are reciprocally related; hence, neither can be properly understood without at least implicit reference to the other. But to make that point clear, he needed a key insight into the nature of reality that could serve as common ground or a bridge between religion and science.

In my view Teilhard had that key insight fairly early in life. That is, Teilhard intuitively realized that the world was like a "burning bush" (Exod 3:4), bursting with energy from a transcendent source, a divine plenitude.[2] But, if that is the case, then the world is full of life and energy. Thus the world is not a cosmic machine with purely mechanical parts or members, but a vital network of dynamically interrelated parts or members, each endowed with an internal life-principle or some form of subjectivity. Yet this way of looking at reality does not fit well with either the traditional metaphysics of Christian theology or with the presuppositions of contemporary natural science. For example, in its doctrinal statements, the Roman Catholic Church regularly employs the philosophy and theology of Thomas Aquinas, who in his *Summa theologiae* laid out in impressive detail the objectively ordered plan of creation provided by an omniscient and omnipotent creator God. But in a world governed by universal laws and principles, the unique individuality of each creature—and, in human beings, the power of personal self-expression—is marginalized. Similarly, many natural scientists up to the present day are uncomfortable with the notion of subjectivity or spontaneity in their analysis of the workings of the world of nature because it seems to call into question the universality of their mathematically based theories about how things work. Teilhard, however, intuitively

---

[2] Pierre Teilhard de Chardin, *The Heart of Matter*, trans. René Hague (New York: Harcourt, Brace, and Co., 1978), 15–24.

saw a spontaneity or unpredictability in the way that nature operates from moment to moment. Hence, he adopted the notion of the "inside" as opposed to the "outside" of everything that exists, even something as small as a grain of sand. In this way he tried to take note of spontaneity as well as objectivity in his formulation of the laws of nature. But as a result, his understanding of the God-world relationship was more process oriented and future oriented than was customary for most Christian systematic theologians of his day.

Here one might object that Teilhard does not regularly use the technical terms *subjectivity* and *objectivity* in describing the cosmic process in *The Human Phenomenon* and elsewhere. But as I see it, they are there by implication. How else is one to explain the "inside" (as opposed to the "outside") of even a grain of sand? What is the hidden energy source for the world as a "burning bush"? Furthermore, Teilhard explained final causality as an internal principle at work within an entity, rather than as an objective principle in a world constituted by objective cause-effect relations, as in the standard textbooks for systematic theology of his day. Before dealing with Teilhard's master work *The Human Phenomenon* in greater detail, however, I review in the first two parts of this chapter how ancient and medieval theologians and then early modern natural scientists were in different ways so focused on conceptual precision in their thinking that they basically lost sight of the key role of subjectivity—the hidden principle of change or potentiality in their systems of explanation.

Ancient and Medieval Philosophy: A World of Universals

The basic understanding of the God-world relationship in the Hebrew and Christian Bible is grounded in subjectivity or, more precisely, intersubjectivity. God and human beings interact in something like an I-Thou relationship. God is pictured in the scriptures as either pleased or displeased by the behavior of the chosen people; Jews and Christians, as a result, feel either confident or anxious about their ongoing personal relationship to God. When the message of the Gospel was shared with the first-century Gentile world, however, the early Christians were confronted with a radically impersonal worldview dominated by universal laws and principles that worked fatalistically. For example, most Gentiles believed that their lives were determined by the three Fates: Clotho spun the thread of human fate; Lachesis dispensed it; Atopos cut the thread, thus determining the individual's moment of death. Others turned instead to various philosophical schemes for explanation of the origin of the world and the meaning of human life. Prominent among the philosophers thus consulted were Plato and his most distinguished pupil, Aristotle. Plato distinguished between the eternal unchanging world of transcendent forms (universal concepts) and the ever-changing world of sensible reality, and claimed that life in this world is intelligible only if reference is regularly made to these transcendent forms or structures to give everything its proper place.[3] Aristotle, more empirically oriented than Plato, claimed instead that the transcendent forms did not exist somewhere apart from the entities of this world, as Plato maintained, but were embodied in physical entities as their unchanging principles of existence and activity or their substantial forms.[4] Not fate, as with ordinary people, but necessity in another form—formal logic—thus governed for well-educated, philosophically oriented Gentiles their understanding of the world and the deeper meaning of life.

Early apologists for the Christian faith to the non-Christian world like WP Martyr, therefore, resorted to the language of these Greek and Roman philosophers to show the rational credibility of their defense of Christian belief. Hence, their presentation of the Christian faith inevitably became more

---

[3] Plato, *The Republic*, trans. Francis MaDonald Cornford (New York: Oxford University Press, 1962), Bk. VI 509D–511B—Bk. VII 514A–521B (The Analogy of the Cave).

[4] Aristotle, *Metaphysics*, trans. Hippocrates G. Apostle (Grinnell, IA: Peripatetic Press, 1979), 1069a–1069b.

impersonal and, as a result, somewhat abstract, in contrast to the much more interpersonal understanding of the God-world relationship world stemming from their reading of the Hebrew and Christian scriptures. At the end of the nineteenth century the celebrated Lutheran Church historian Adolf Harnack called attention to this discrepancy between the language of scripture and the language of the early Christian apologists like Justin Martyr. Accordingly, he wrote a two-volume work, *The Expansion of Christianity in the First Three Centuries*, in which he claimed that the message of Jesus as presented in the Gospels and the writings of St. Paul was significantly changed, perhaps even betrayed, by this "Hellenization" of Christian belief.[5] Further research on the writings of the Greek and Roman Fathers of the church has made clear that Harnack significantly overstated his case. Christianity was not thereby reduced to Gnosticism, a religion only for the intellectual elite, not ordinary people. Yet in fairness to Harnack, the decrees of the early ecumenical councils of the church (Nicaea in 325, Constantinople in 381, Ephesus in 431, and Chalcedon in 451) all employed philosophical concepts not found in scripture (nature, person, substance, and so on) to define the doctrine of the Trinity, the divinity of the Holy Spirit, and the divinity as well as the humanity of Jesus as God Incarnate.

Aquinas, Bonaventure, and Others

Thomas Aquinas, perhaps the most brilliant philosopher/theologian in the medieval period, was well acquainted with the metaphorical language of prominent neo-Platonic thinkers like Proclus, Simplicius, and Pseudo-Dionysius, but he preferred the more abstract and logical categories of Aristotle's philosophy for his own articulation of the Christian belief system, above all in his most comprehensive work, the *Summa theologiae*. As

---

[5] Adolph Harnack, *The Mission and Expansion of Christianity in the First Three Centuries*, trans. J. Moffatt (New York: G.P. Putnam, 1908), 1:24–35.

a result, Aquinas worked out his theology in a mental world dominated by universal concepts and objective logic. He was, of course, still a man of deep feeling, as is evident from examining his reverential, feeling-oriented hymns for the exposition of the holy Eucharist. But in his more systematic reflections on Christian dogma, he evidently felt more at home thinking within the abstract framework of Aristotelian philosophy than in dealing with all the complexities of an interpersonal relationship with God that ordinary human beings in the Middle Ages faced on a regular basis. As an example of his very careful thinking, Aquinas claimed that Plato's transcendental ideas are located first of all in the mind of God as Creator of the universe; second, in the substantial forms of the physical entities in this world; and third, in the minds of human beings through an unconscious mental abstraction on their part from the limiting conditions of matter.[6] This explanation was an intellectual tour de force on his part in dealing with the thorny question of where universal concepts are located and how they are usually operative in human life. But this line of thought still presents an abstraction from sensible reality, that is, the lives of individuals. So, more than he perhaps was aware, in working out his theology Aquinas was thinking largely in terms of a world of universal concepts.

Admittedly, other philosopher-theologians in the medieval period were more sensitive to the concrete reality of the entities of this world and their individual differences from one another, even though they too shared with Aquinas a worldview dominated by universal concepts. Bonaventure, for example, emphasized the love of God for creatures.[7] But for God to love someone or something, God must love that creature as an individual entity in its own right rather than simply as a component

---

[6] Frederick Copleston, SJ, *A History of Philosophy,* vol. 2, part 1 (Garden City, NY: Doubleday, 1962), 175–76.

[7] Ilia Delio, *The Emergent Christ: Exploring the Meaning of Catholic in an Evolutionary Universe* (Maryknoll, NY: Orbis Books, 2012), 36–39.

in God's master plan for the world of creation. Another Franciscan theologian, Duns Scotus, claimed that human beings have a kind of sense-knowledge (or sensory cognition) of other entities, as well as of themselves, as unique individuals. But, somewhat ironically, Scotus held that human beings have this individualized knowledge of themselves and other entities only in virtue of still another universal form or concept, namely, *haecceitas* or "thisness."[8] Finally, a third Franciscan friar, William of Ockham, solved the problem of universal concepts by reducing them simply to the ordinary names of things, that is, the words human beings conventionally use to classify different individual entities in their dealings with them.[9] But even Ockham was still thinking in relatively abstract terms, namely, what can be said about all entities of a given class. For him, as well as for Aquinas, Bonaventure, and Duns Scotus, subjectivity (understood as an individual entity's innate power to change itself and the world around it) was reserved to God as Creator of the universe. Human beings as creatures instead lived within a world governed by preexistent laws and principles. In the course of their lives they made various "accidental" changes as needed. But the basic pattern of life in this world remained unchanged for them and for all their contemporaries.

Early Modern Philosophy: The Quest for Certitude

This sense of living in a relatively unchanging and highly predictable world changed dramatically at the beginning of the early modern period in Western history. The God-centered medieval worldview was challenged by the Renaissance with

---

[8] Mary Beth Ingham and Mechthil Dreyer, *The Philosophical Vision of John Duns Scotus: An Introduction* (Washington, DC: Catholic University of America Press, 2004), 25–31, 101–16; Copleston, *A History of Philosophy*, vol. 2, part 2, 216.

[9] W. T. Jones, *A History of Western Philosophy*, vol. 2, *The Medieval Mind*, 2nd ed. (New York: Harcourt, Brace, and World, 1969), 321.

its new focus on humanism, above all, as depicted in the Greek and Roman classics; not God but the human being was the center of attention. But this was only the first major change for Christians living at the start of the early modern era of Western civilization. The printing press was invented by Johannes Gutenberg in the 1440s, with a consequent jump in literacy even among ordinary people in Western Europe. In 1492, Columbus discovered the New World, and voyages of discovery to other parts of the world were undertaken shortly thereafter. Luther in 1517 challenged the authority of the pope and bishops in settling issues of church doctrine and practice, thereby initiating the Protestant Reformation with all its further consequences for the political order in Western Europe. So it was not surprising that reflective individuals like René Descartes found themselves searching for a safe starting point for their studies in philosophy. In addition, Descartes was a mathematician who enjoyed the logical certitude that came from setting forth a set of interconnected axioms as unquestionably true and then thinking through their logical consequences.

But in following out that line of thought, Descartes did not begin with rational arguments for the existence of God, as Aquinas did in his *Summa theologiae*; rather, Descartes began with reflection on his own human existence here and now.[10] From the indisputable fact of his own existence, he was then able to deduce the existence of God, since only God could have implanted in his mind and heart the idea of infinity. Everything else in his day-to-day experience of self and world was finite and limited. So, if he found himself thinking about God as Infinite Being, where did it come from if not from God via what Descartes called an "innate idea"?[11] Then, confident that God exists, Descartes could be equally confident of the real existence of the

---

[10] René Descartes, "Meditations on First Philosophy, II," in *The Philosophical Works of Descartes,* vol. 1, trans. Elizabeth Haldane and G.R.T. Ross (Cambridge, UK: Cambridge University Press, 1931), 150.

[11] Descartes, "Meditations on First Philosophy, III," in ibid., 160.

world around himself since God as perfect being would not trick him into believing what was factually untrue, or simply an illusion.[12] Hence, Descartes ended with an objective understanding of the God-world relationship that closely resembled the work of Aquinas and other medieval Scholastic thinkers; but he began with something new, namely, explicit recognition of his own individual subjectivity as the necessary starting point for that same objective God-world relationship. He also broke with the medieval tradition in his further contention that universal concepts like the classical notion of substantial form or essence of things are only imperfect mental representations of those same things.[13] So, while Descartes was still basically a realist confident in his knowledge of the external world, in other ways he introduced uncertainty into his knowledge of the world around him. Could he really trust the veracity of his "representations" of the objective things of this world?

John Locke and David Hume

The English physician turned philosopher John Locke read Descartes's philosophical reflections and admired their logical coherence. But, given his experience as a practicing physician, he was more empirically oriented than Descartes. In his book *An Essay Concerning Human Understanding* he employed what he called the "historical, plain method" of introspection into the workings of his own mind as he reflected on and organized the data of experience.[14] But for the same reason he implicitly shared with Descartes the belief that we only know our own ideas or mental representations of things, not their full physical reality. Furthermore, he tended toward reductionism in his

---

[12] Descartes, "Meditations on First Philosophy, VI," in ibid., 191–92.

[13] Descartes, "Meditations on First Philosophy, III," in ibid., 160–61.

[14] John Locke, *An Essay concerning Human Understanding*, ed. Peter Nidditch (Oxford, UK: Clarendon Press, 1975), 44.

organization of ideas. That is, he assumed that complex ideas are nothing more than the adroit combination of simple ideas.[15] Simple ideas are derived immediately from direct sense experience; more complex ideas, like the abstract properties of things and their relation to one another, are more the work of the mind in comparing and contrasting simple ideas with one another. He also had more confidence in those qualities or properties of things that can be quantitatively measured (size, weight, figure, and so on) as opposed to other secondary qualities of things that cannot be mathematically ordered (colors, sounds, tastes).[16]

As a result he was even more of an abstract thinker than Descartes. He could not be sure, given this distinction between the primary and secondary qualities of things, whether he really comprehended the essence or nature of any of the things that he perceived in sense experience. So he used the expression "nominal essence" to describe what he learned from the combination of simple ideas in his own mind.[17] But then he had to admit that he had no real knowledge of the form or substance of things except as the unknowable substrate or theoretical foundation for a collection of primary and secondary qualities.[18] Finally, he could not be certain of the objective reality of cause-and-effect relations that seemed to be taking place in the world around him. For example, if all that human beings experience is a succession of sense perceptions,[19] is it really physical heat that causes wax to become fluid or is it only the idea of heat that regularly gives rise to the idea of wax as something fluid? In this way Locke prepared the way for the devastating critique of classical metaphysics and the classical laws of nature in the philosophy of David Hume.

In *A Treatise on Human Nature* Hume distinguished between ideas and impressions. Ideas are derived directly from

---

[15] Ibid., 8.
[16] Ibid., 134–43.
[17] Ibid., 453.
[18] Ibid., 95.
[19] Ibid., 325.

sense perception; impressions are the result of further mental reflection on ideas.[20] For example, if the idea of smoke is consistently linked with the idea of fire in one's sense experience, then one gains the impression of a cause-and-effect relation at work in the world around oneself—but one cannot then prove that this impression is de facto true.[21] It may or may not correspond to the way that cause-effect relations actually work in the natural world. Human beings are thus trapped within mental worlds of their own construction. Furthermore, Hume could not be sure that he himself existed as an unchanging self that observes the flow of images and ideas within his conscious experience.[22] So in the hands of David Hume, Descartes's turn to his own individual subjectivity as starting point for philosophical reflection on the nature of reality ended in total skepticism about the possibility of objective truth and genuine certitude in human understanding of self, God, and world. Thus, a response had to be made by someone who took Hume's critical approach to reality seriously but still found a way to circumvent it and thus restore the possibility of truth and objectivity in human discourse, above all, in doing scientific research.

Immanuel Kant's Copernican Revolution

The German philosopher Immanuel Kant responded to that challenge. He had academic training in the natural sciences, notably astronomy, and was well read in the rationalist philosophies of Christian Wolff and Gottfried Leibniz. Hence, when he read Hume's *Treatise on Human Nature,* he recognized immediately how Hume's understanding of the principle of causality as simply a subjective habit of mind, a tendency to think of one idea as the cause of another, destroyed any

---

[20] David Hume, *A Treatise of Human Nature*, ed. L. A. Selby-Bigge (Oxford, UK: Clarendon Press, 1967), 1.

[21] Ibid., 88.

[22] Ibid., 207–8, 253.

rational basis for objective laws of nature grounded in cause-effect relations. At the same time, it was already clear to him from reading the works of Wolff and Leibniz that a priori, or purely logical, philosophical reflection on the nature of reality cannot ever be fully verified in actual human experience. So he had to find a way to make empirically based, sound judgments about the flow of sense data within his consciousness. His solution was brilliant, equivalent to a second Copernican Revolution in thinking about the nature of reality.

Instead of claiming that true and certain human knowledge inevitably conforms to preexistent laws of nature, he proposed that the data of human sense experience conform to preexistent laws of cognition within the human mind.[23] In other words human beings have insight into what they themselves are already prepared to recognize and understand in terms of the way their minds are antecedently structured. But, argued Kant, since all human minds operate in basically the same way, what each one finds in experience will be basically the same as what everyone else finds, for example, laws of cause and effect, substance-accident relations, and simultaneity or the coexistence of entities with one another. He thereby opened up an even bigger problem. For, according to Kant, the laws of the mind only apply to the data of sense-experience or the *phenomena*, not to physical entities existing in their own right within extra-mental reality, what Kant calls the *noumena*.[24] So human beings will never be able to prove rationally the existence of God or to know with certitude the extra-mental reality of the human self and the world of nature. The notions of God, the personal self, and the world of nature were thus for Kant only regulative ideas for ordering one's life, especially with respect to the accepted moral order within civil society. Their extra-mental reality, however, can only be asserted, not empirically validated.

---

[23] Immanuel Kant, *Critique of Pure Reason,* trans. Norman Kemp Smith (New York: St. Martin's Press, 1956), B xiii. B refers to the second edition of the *Critique.*

[24] Ibid., B xxvi–xxvii.

In many ways, of course, Kant's approach to human cognition simply reflected the already existing methodology of most natural scientists of his own day in dealing with the empirical data of their scientific research. One does not begin with metaphysics, an a priori scheme for how God, the self, and the world of nature are related to one another. Rather, one begins with careful observation and analysis of the data of one's subjective experience of reality. Then one looks for persistent patterns in the way that one perceives contemporary events and the regular succession of events vis-à-vis one another. Eventually one comes up with a provisional theory as to why things happen the way that they do in one's experience. Finally, one shares with other scientists working in the same field the results of one's research and asks them to test one's hypothesis in their own scientific research. Kant, of course, was confident that his theory was correct because in *The Critique of Pure Reason* he linked his basic concepts for the organization of sense experience to the logical forms of judgment in Aristotle's philosophy.[25] Here, however, he himself was still thinking too much in a priori fashion about the way that the human mind works. Further research in the relatively new fields of anthropology and sociology made abundantly clear that human beings do not perceive reality and think exactly alike and that one's culture as well as one's personal biases affect how one first sees and then understands reality.

Post-Kantian Developments

Paradoxically, Kant's rejection of classical metaphysics in *The Critique of Pure Reason* soon gave rise to new forms of metaphysics that focused on cosmology, the way the world works, as opposed to epistemology, the way that the human mind works. For example, the three so-called German idealists

---

[25] Ibid., B 95; Aristotle, *Metaphysics,* 1017a.

(Fichte, Schelling, and Hegel) transferred Kant's focus on the creativity of the human mind to an alleged, higher-order creativity already at work in the cosmic process. Fichte, for example, postulated that the workings of the human mind are based on an underlying dialectical activity at work in the world at large.[26] Hence, if every thesis or individual statement about the nature of reality can be contradicted by its antithesis or logical opposite (for example, Being vs. Nothing), so that one is driven to think of the dialectical unity of the two statements in terms of a synthesis, then this movement from thesis to antithesis to synthesis reflects the way that nature itself works. Reality is a process of becoming; everything is continually undergoing change. The ongoing structure and mode of operation of the world is not predetermined by God, as in classical metaphysics, but is instead evolving toward greater order and complexity in virtue of an internal principle of self-organization in three stages that are repeated over and over again.

Schelling and Hegel further specified that this internal principle of self-organization within the cosmic process is either God (for Schelling) or Absolute Spirit (for Hegel). In both cases God or Absolute Spirit evolves along with the world.[27] In terms of Fichte's threefold dialectical scheme, for example, God is the thesis; the world is the antithesis; God and the world evolving together are the synthesis, the ultimate reason for the cosmic process. A generation later Karl Marx challenged the priority of spirit over matter in the worldviews of Fichte, Schelling, and Hegel; instead, he proposed an ongoing interplay between matter and spirit in the relations of human beings both with one another and with the world of nature. Thus spirit is emergent

---

[26] See "Second Introduction," *Fichte: Science of Knowledge*, trans. Peter Heath and John Lachs (New York: Appleton-Century-Crofts, 1970), 40.

[27] *Schellings Werke*, vol. 4, ed. Manfred Schröter (Munich: C. H. Beck, 1958), 223–309 *(The Nature of Human Freedom)*; G. W. F. Hegel, *Phenomenology of the Spirit*, ed. Johannes Hoffmeister (Hamburg: Felix Meiner, 1952).

out of matter rather than matter emergent out of preexistent spirit:

> According to Marx's "consistent naturalism or human-ism," the emergence of the human spirit takes place at a late stage in the evolution of man. It is a product of the power of development immanent in the "species-life," generated and impelled by man's life in society, the development which accounts for constant human growth and ever new achievements. All events are equally natural; in particular, social, moral, and spiritual life, all that is truly creative and powerful in man, belongs to the natural order of things, as much as man's biological life.[28]

For Marx, then, matter is a source of novelty and change in its own right. It does not need the infusion of spirit from God or some other cosmic source outside itself to evolve in a given direction. It possesses an inbuilt potentiality for self-organization and growth.[29]

Despite their obvious differences in worldview, therefore, both the German Idealists and Karl Marx were experimenting with a new approach to reality, namely, the priority of subjectivity over objectivity, potentiality over actuality in understanding how the world works. The German Idealists emphasized either the subjectivity of God or the subjectivity of the human mind in shaping human history and the world of nature. Marx emphasized the intersubjective relations of human beings both in dealing with one another and in their common efforts to deal effectively with the forces of nature. Yet none of these three authors offered a religiously inspired worldview that would be simultaneously compatible both with

---

[28] A. Z. Jordan, *The Evolution of Dialectical Materialism* (London: Macmillan, 1967), 61.

[29] Karl Marx, "Critique of Hegel's Dialectic and Philosophy in General," *Writings of the Young Marx on Philosophy and Society*, trans. L. D. Easton and K. H. Guddat (Indianapolis, IN: Hackett, 1997), 314–37.

scientific knowledge of the natural world and with the traditional Christian understanding of the God-world relationship.
Given his own training in philosophy and theology as well as
natural science, the French Jesuit Pierre Teilhard de Chardin
was thus in a privileged position to provide a much needed,
religiously inspired, and yet scientifically based worldview.

The Cosmic Vision of Teilhard de Chardin

As mentioned earlier in this chapter Chardin was heavily influenced in his overall outlook on life by the mindset or enduring
preoccupation of his parents: his mother, the devout Roman
Catholic; his father, a naturalist with a special interest in geology. Even in his early home life, therefore, Teilhard must have
been aware of the competing interests of natural science, with
its strong empirical approach to life, and of religion, with its
equally strong focus on the intangible life of the spirit along
with an unwavering belief in the reality of the supernatural. His
outlook on life was also much influenced by what he learned as
a student at the Jesuit College of Mongré in Villefranche-sur-
Saon. In fact, he admired the work of the Jesuit fathers at the
college so much that he chose to become a member of the order
at the age of eighteen. As part of his preparation for ordination
to the priesthood, he studied philosophy on the Isle of Jersey
in the English Channel and theology at Hastings on the south
coast of England. But his interest in natural science did not die
out. He read with keen interest Henri Bergson's book *Creative
Evolution*,[30] and in the years between his prescribed studies in
philosophy and theology he taught physics and chemistry at
the Jesuit College in Cairo, Egypt.

After ordination to the priesthood he worked for two years
in the department of paleontology at the National Museum
of Natural History in Paris. This work was interrupted by the

---

[30] Henri Bergson, *Creative Evolution*, trans. Arthur Mitchell (New
York: Modern Library, 1944).

outbreak of the First World War, when he volunteered to serve as a stretcher bearer in the French Army. With the end of the war in 1918 he returned to academic life, earning a doctorate in natural science at the Sorbonne and afterward teaching geology at the Catholic Institute in Paris. In 1923, while still a faculty member at the Catholic Institute, he made his first trip to China as part of an expedition in search of human fossil remains. After this year in the field he returned to Paris and resumed teaching duties at the Catholic Institute. In the meantime he had written and circulated privately a couple of doctrinally suspect essays on original sin from an evolutionary perspective.[31] When his religious superiors learned of this indiscretion on Teilhard's part, they relieved him of his teaching duties at the Catholic Institute and "exiled" him to China to do further work in paleontology. During these later years in China he began work on his major work, *The Human Phenomenon*. In what follows I present a summary and modest critique of that book with its special focus on evolution as based on empirically oriented principles of Becoming.[32]

Introductory Comments

In an introductory "Author's Note," for example, Teilhard explained that his book was not a text in metaphysics, namely, "a system of ontological and causal relations among the elements of the universe" (1), but a "hyperphysics" (2), an empirically grounded theory for the way that the cosmic process has developed over time. For this purpose Teilhard set forth two working presuppositions: "The first is the primacy accorded to the psyche and to thought in the stuff of the universe. And the second is the 'biological' value attributed to the social fact around us" (2). Teilhard gave primacy to psyche and thought rather

---

[31] For further details, see David Grumett and Paul Bentley, "Teilhard de Chardin, Original Sin, and the Six Propositions," *Zygon* 53, no. 2 (June 2018): 303–30.

[32] I give the page number of the text of *The Human Phenomenon* in parentheses wherever needed.

than inanimate matter as the basic "stuff" of the universe, presumably because he had in mind the notion of subjectivity as the vital source or immanent principle of potentiality in the workings of the cosmic process. For, if the cosmic process is in fact continually evolving, never exactly the same from one moment to the next, it seems logical that an underlying principle of subjectivity is invisibly at work—not only in the minds and hearts of human beings but also, in some measure, within other living creatures as well. Likewise, Teilhard linked "biology" with "the social fact around us" because human beings are in constant interaction with one another and their social context or environment in order to survive and prosper. Interaction with other entities in one's environment then provides a human being with new energy for growth and development, whereas a human being existing apart from other living things tends to lose energy and to become lethargic or even despondent.

Then, in the prologue of *The Human Phenomenon*, which Teilhard entitles "Seeing," Teilhard claims that "the whole of life lies in seeing" (3). Inanimate things do not "see" anything. Only if they are alive, are in some sense subjects of experience with a feeling-level sensitivity to their environment and an innate ability to respond to what is going on in the environment, do they "see" other entities and feel the impulse to move toward union with these others so as to support and be supported by them in their common struggle for survival within the cosmic process. Teilhard also claims that human beings "see" or understand the world in terms of their own mental concepts or principles as products of their imagination. As a result, they find themselves living partly in a self-made world, yet subject to ongoing constraints not only from the world of nature but from their own previous actions and decisions (4). Teilhard, however, then goes on to say that human beings are "the center of construction of the universe" (4), "the axis and arrow of evolution" (7). Human beings are thus the "mind" of the cosmic process, shaping its overall evolution. Here, in my judgment, Teilhard overstates his case. Admittedly, human beings, as the only known intelligent species, have a strong influence on the way that evolution works on earth. But the earth is only a part of the solar system, and the solar system is only a small part of the Milky Way galaxy, which is itself just one of millions, if not billions, of galaxies in the universe. Hence, Teilhard is unwittingly substituting a small part of the universe for the meaning and value of the whole of the universe. It may be a very important part for the human understanding of the universe, but it is still only a part. I shall return to this point at the end of the chapter in critiquing Teilhard's linkage of the overall goal of the cosmic process with the Cosmic Christ of traditional Christian eschatology.

Prelife

The first two parts of *The Human Phenomenon* are titled "Prelife" and "Life." In Prelife, Teilhard describes the slow growth in the overall structure and complexity of the earth before the initial emergence of primitive forms of life. At the same time he is implicitly laying out the foundational concepts and organizing principles of his "hyperphysics." For example, he first writes, "Plurality, unity and energy are the three aspects of matter" (12). That is, matter is not something continuous and everywhere the same but is broken up into tiny bits that are different from one another—and yet, these mini-entities are dynamically related to one another to constitute the complex unity of an organism, however large or small. Energy is "the measure of what is transferred from one atom to another in the process of their [organic] transformations" (13). The material world can thus be described in three ways: system, totum, and quantum. As a *system* the material world is a unity-in-diversity of dynamically interrelated parts or members. As a *totum* the material world is an open-ended process that keeps the same basic mode of operation but still never repeats itself exactly from moment to moment. Finally, as a *quantum* the material universe is a totality or whole that is both the sum of its parts and more than the sum of its parts, something existing in its own right independently of its parts or members (14–16). The unity of the whole is reflected in the unity of each part or member, just as the unity of each part or member is reflected in the evolving unity of the whole (17). Yet, writes Teilhard, none of this could happen without a psychic dimension or elementary form of subjectivity at work in entities even at the stage of prelife. For inanimate entities do not have the power to dynamically interrelate; their only unity is that of an aggregate, a combination of material parts that exists for a short time and then breaks up under the pressure of external environmental factors. Only if the component parts or members of the whole are dynamically interrelated does the totality or whole survive in an often hostile environment.

To account for the ongoing unity of an organism under external pressure, Teilhard introduces a new term, "the inside of things." He concedes that physicists by and large deal with the outside or physical appearance of things. But in his view, "deep within ourselves, through a rent or tear, an 'interior' appears at the heart of beings" (24). Hence, "coextensive with its outside, everything has an inside" (24). In explanation of this point he makes three observations. First, both the inside and the outside of things are composed of smaller "atomic" parts or members. Second, both the inside and outside of things possess an underlying unity. Third, that underlying unity is sustained by energy coming from the whole as an innate energy-source (26). Hence, growth in consciousness and growth in outward complexity "are merely the two connected faces or parts of a single phenomenon" (27), that is, the way the world works from moment to moment.

Admittedly, at the level of physics and chemistry these psycho-physical centers of consciousness are very numerous, with little interconnection between them; hence, at the level of physics and chemistry these atomic entities exhibit no empirically recognizable signs of life or consciousness. At higher levels of complexity and centricity in biology, however, these centers of awareness are more self-aware and more spontaneous in their relation to one another, both of which are infallible signs of life and consciousness (28). Accordingly, the outside and the inside of things are both empowered by one and the same energy in two different forms: *tangential energy* to connect these mini-entities to one another outwardly, and *radial energy* to move each of them singly and all of them together "in the direction of an ever more complex and centered state, toward what is ahead" (30). Hence, for Teilhard, the foundational principle of self-organization for the cosmic process is what he calls the law of complexification-consciousness: the more complex an entity is on the "outside," the more centered and thus conscious it is on the "inside." Finally, in the last chapter of "Prelife," entitled "The Juvenile Earth," Teilhard describes the condition of the earth on the eve of the appearance of life. From the outside he notes the movement from the "crystallizing world," that is, horizontal networks of similarly constituted entities, to the "polymerizing world," in which smaller and simpler entities combine to form larger and more complex entities. From the inside, however, he notes how this slow growth in size and complexity produces "an interdependent mass of infinitesimal centers structurally interconnected by their conditions of origin and their development" (38).

Life

In the first chapter of "Life," entitled "The Appearance of Life," Teilhard claims that these masses of psycho-physical mini-entities become cells, "the natural grain of life," when they fold in on one another and become enclosed within a protective membrane (43). Even more important, he claims that "the cell can only be *understood* (that is, incorporated into a coherent system of the universe) when it is historically based, part of an evolutionary line of development (43). In other words, a cell is "something born," that is, something new, not something mechanically reproduced. It has a unique origin and a similarly unique, irreversible path of future development. It is alive because it has an unpredictable spontaneity within it all through the stages of life from birth to death. Yet, despite its individual uniqueness, the cell does not exist in isolation from

other cells; however thin it might have been, the initial grouping of cells spread out over the face of the earth could neither
have established nor maintained itself without some network
of influence and exchange that made it biologically *connected*
as a whole (54).

In the next chapter Teilhard analyzes the expansion of life
from this primitive layer of organic life into ever-larger clusters
of cells through a series of successive interrelated movements:
first, multiplication of the original cells; second, diversification of
cells through change of form in reproduction (above all, sexual
reproduction as opposed to asexual reproduction); third, the
grouping of cells so as to constitute higher-order cells with an
autonomous center, equivalent to a primitive soul or organizing
principle for the other lower-order cells in the group; and finally,
orthogenesis or directionality. With directionality the focus of
attention shifts from the cell as an individual entity to its role as
a single link in the ongoing transmission of a life-form (67–68).
Accordingly, spread over the earth, life in all its forms is "a single, gigantic organism" (68). Yet this initial thrust of life on this
earth is soon diversified into phyla (different forms of organic
life) and then into verticils (further subdivisions of a phylum in
a given direction). Teilhard calls this ongoing diversification of
life-forms "the tree of life," with special attention to one branch,
the mammals, of which the primates and in particular the human
species are members. Finally, in the last chapter of "Life," he
comes to the conclusion that "the 'impetus' of the world revealed
by the great thrust of consciousness can only have its ultimate
source, and it can only find an explanation for its irreversible
advance toward a higher psyche, in the existence of some kind of
interior principle of movement" (97), namely, thought, the power
to transcend the limiting conditions of matter in and through
growing self-awareness (106).

For Teilhard, then, the cosmic process on this earth is not
machine-like in its operation, with unchanging laws and
universally applicable principles. Rather, as a gigantic organism, it is suffused with subjectivity, understood as the built-in
capacity for spontaneous change and ongoing adaptation to

unforeseen circumstances. Most of the natural scientists of his time (and many natural scientists to this day) have rejected Teilhard's insertion of subjectivity into the workings of the cosmic process because it interferes with the objective workings of the mathematically formulated laws and principles that have proven to be so fruitful in the past for human beings to understand and control the workings of nature to their own advantage. But in recent years other philosopher-scientists have implicitly endorsed the notion of subjectivity as a universal principle at work in physical reality. James Lovelock, for example, proposed the Gaia hypothesis, namely, that the living and nonliving parts of the earth form a complex interactive system that can be thought of as a single organism.[33] Other earth-system scientists, who study the physical composition of the earth and its atmosphere at different geological levels, maintain that human beings have been and continue to be dynamically interconnected with all other living and non-living entities in the geological history of the planet.[34] But, to the best of my knowledge, none of these philosopher-scientists makes the further claim that the progressive growth of the brain in primates—especially in human beings—coincides with the orthogenesis or underlying directionality of the entire cosmic process on earth. Yet this is the theme of Part Three of *The Human Phenomenon*, namely, "Thought."

Thought

In the first chapter of Part Three, Teilhard sketches what he calls the "hominization" of the individual human being. An

[33] James Lovelock, *Gaia: A New Look at Life on Earth* (Oxford, UK: Oxford University Press, 1979).

[34] Cf., for example, Bruno Latour, *Facing Gaia: Eight Lectures on the New Climatic Regime* (Cambridge, UK: Polity Press, 2017); William E. Connolly, *Facing the Planetary: Entangled Humanism and the Politics of Swarming* (Durham, NC: Duke University Press, 2017); Amitav Ghosh, *The Great Derangement: Climate Change and the Unthinkable* (Chicago: University of Chicago Press, 2016).

individual human being becomes an "I" in that it turns in on itself and makes itself an object of self-reflection (110). Insofar as it then recognizes its own value and significance, it becomes a person (116). At the same time the individual human being is contributing to the hominization of the species, its division into different races, different cultures, and different individual behavior patterns, all of them contributing to the psychic growth of the species (122). At this point Teilhard introduces a new term, the *noosphere,* the sphere of mind that directly influences the further development and growth of not only the human species but of all the other life-forms on earth (122–25). In and through the presence and activity of human beings in dealing with one another, other plant and animal species, and the material conditions of life on this planet, the earth "finds its soul" (124). There is some parallel here to what some earth scientists have described as the emergent Anthropocene era of the earth's geology, replacing the Holocene era that began eleven thousand years ago. In the Holocene era human beings lived more or less in harmony with the prevailing conditions of life on earth; in this emergent Anthropocene era humans are said to be irrevocably altering the conditions of life on earth. The Industrial Revolution of the nineteenth century and, above all, the explosion of the first atomic bomb at the end of the Second World War, are seen as examples of human beings dramatically changing the conditions of life for everyone and everything else on the face of the earth.

But, whereas Teilhard envisions human beings as taking the lead in the ongoing evolution of the cosmic process, the proponents of the Anthropocene theory of geological evolution claim that human beings share this responsibility with many other nonhuman causal agencies. Similarly, Donna Haraway resituates humans and nonhumans alike within the common ground of "Terra," and thus as interrelated "Terrans," or "companion species."[35] But, while Haraway and other earth-science thinkers

---

[35] Donna J. Haraway, *Staying with the Trouble: Making Kin in the Chthulucene* (Durham, NC: Duke University Press, 2016), 175.

envision the cosmic process in secular this-worldly terms, Teilhard envisions the cosmic process as destined to achieve a transcendent end, an Omega Point that is supra-personal. For this reason alone Teilhard has to claim that the axis of the evolutionary process on this earth passes through the noo-sphere or world of thought generated by human beings in their interpersonal dealings with one another over the centuries.

Telihard's argument runs as follows. Charles Darwin and other early proponents of evolution through natural selection looked at evolution from a purely objective standpoint, as something taking place in the world of nature, but not in themselves as likewise subject to evolution (153). Only when they eventually grasped how their own reflections on the nature of reality were gradually evolving did they belatedly realize that they themselves were "nothing else than evolution become conscious of itself" (154). But, as an unexpected consequence of general acceptance of the fact of evolution, modern human beings have tended to be uneasy about the future in a way that their predecessors, living in the relatively stable world of the medieval and early modern period of human history, were not. For, faced with the evolving character of life all around them, human beings must inevitably ask themselves about the meaning of their own lives and what will happen to them at the end of their lives. According to Teilhard, this anxiety about the future can only be laid to rest if human beings believe in a higher form of existence, a *superlife*, something that is within reach if human beings remain true to the particular pattern of evolution that has brought them to their current situation (163).

Superlife

"Superlife," then is the theme of Part Four of *The Human Phenomenon*. But what is superlife, and how does one achieve it, starting from the present moment? Teilhard first makes clear that superlife is never achieved by individuals acting in isolation from one another (167–68). Rather, it happens collectively. Simply by reason of their growth in numbers and their increased communication with one another as a result of modern technology, human beings are being drawn into an "energetic concentration of consciousnesses" (170). But then, given the ongoing connection between complexity and consciousness, human beings find themselves likewise involved in ever more complex social configurations (172). They end up co-creating a collective reality called humanity, which is just as objective and real as the human beings that make it up (175). In similar fashion modern science seems to be bent on achieving another higher-order collective reality, namely, a humanity actively engaged in the conquest of nature's forces in the service of spirit (176). Thus, the noosphere should be understood as "a single closed system in which each element sees, feels, desires, and suffers for itself the same things at the same time as all the others" (178). But for Teilhard, then, "a new step in the genesis of spirit" is required, namely, the transition from the collective to the hyperpersonal.

What does Teilhard mean by the term *hyperpersonal?* Teilhard first notes that "modern humans are obsessed by the need to depersonalize (or impersonalize) all that they most admire" (183). But, says Teilhard, the Omega Point or goal of the cosmic process should be not something impersonal, but rather "some kind of supreme consciousness," given that evolution evidently represents a gradual growth in complexity and consciousness (183–84). The noosphere, accordingly, is constituted by a vast number of entities, each a center of consciousness. The Omega Point serves as both the totality of these centers of consciousness and their organizing principle. Thus, the Omega Point is a hyperpersonal reality (184). On the principle that "union differentiates" (186), every individual self or center of consciousness is both uniquely itself and an active participant in the reality of the noosphere as a whole. But the noosphere must also take on "a face and a heart, become personified for us" (190). As such, the Omega Point must be "somehow already loving and loveable *right here and now*" (192). So the Omega Point must be centered on a transcendent Person here and now as well as identified with a future cosmic community of centers of consciousness. Teilhard seems to be implicitly thinking here of the Christian doctrine of the mystical body, with the risen Christ as its head and all faithful Christians as its members.[36] But, as I shall indicate in Chapter 3, an alternative Christian explanation of the Omega Point would be the incorporation not only of human beings but all of creation into the eternal life of the Trinity in and through Christ as both a divine person in his own right and the Omega Point of the cosmic process.

Somewhat along the same lines, Teilhard also claims that the end of the world will not be catastrophic, a complete disintegration of everything of value in this world. At least some human beings and perhaps all of humankind will be saved through union with the Omega Point through their own free choice (197). "If there is a future for humanity, it can only be imagined in the direction of some harmonious reconciliation of freedom with what is planned and totalized" (202). As a result, the historical end of the world will take place in two stages. In the first stage the noosphere as a community of centers of consciousness will close in on itself and detach itself from its material matrix, the limiting conditions of external physical life on earth (206). In the second stage the noosphere will divide into two zones. In the first zone many or even most of the individual centers of consciousness will be gathered into an all-embracing cosmic community headed up by Christ as the transcendent Omega Point (207). In the other zone the centers of consciousness will instead be psychologically alienated from one another. The end of the world for these isolated centers of consciousness will be a paroxysm of evil "in a specifically new form" (206). Here, Teilhard might have been thinking of the

---

[36] See Pierre Teilhard de Chardin, "Pantheism and Christianity," in *Christianity and Evolution,* trans. René Hague (New York: Harcourt Brace and Jovanovich, 1971), 56–75. This essay was written in 1923, about the same time as Teilhard started to write *The Human Phenomenon.*

life of the damned in Dante's *Inferno* where extinction instead of continued life in isolation would have been a blessing.

Critique and Conclusion

What is to be said by way of comment and critique of *The Human Phenomenon?* Here I use a metaphor drawn from the New Testament. Jesus tells his listeners: "No one puts new wine into old wineskins; otherwise, the wine will burst the skins, and the wine is lost, and so are the skins; but one puts new wine into fresh wineskins" (Mark 2:22). As I see it, Teilhard tried to pour the new wine of a genuinely evolutionary process-oriented approach to reality into the old wineskin of traditional Christian systematic theology with its emphasis on the preexistent divine plan for the world of creation. Likewise, he ended up pouring his new wine into the old wineskin of early modern natural science, with its focus on empirical objectivity to the exclusion of any kind of subjectivity or spontaneity. Predictably, Teilhard's efforts at a new approach to reality were at first vigorously contested. For example, in the world of natural science it was sharply criticized by a Nobel-prize winner, immunologist Peter Medawar, and by influential geneticist Richard Dawkins. Likewise, in the judgment of church authorities and of his own Jesuit superiors, it verged on heresy and had to be censured and barred from appearing in print. Yet, as time went on, the book was much more positively received by both Christians and non-Christians because it offered hope for the future of the human race, above all to those individuals in Western Europe and elsewhere who had experienced the ravages of World War II.

On balance, therefore, Teilhard's cosmology as set forth in *The Human Phenomenon* and elsewhere deserves a serious hearing, not simply from Christians looking for a new approach to the spiritual life, but also from philosophers of science looking for a new way to explain evolution, the unpredictable way that the physical world keeps changing in adaptation to new environmental conditions. Admittedly, Teilhard could possibly have presented his case better. For example, if he had claimed that his hyperphysics was simply a speculative proposal based on innovative principles of *becoming* rather than on the conventional principles of *being* in classical metaphysics, both theologians and philosophers of science might have taken more time to study his hypothesis more carefully. By claiming that his theory of hyperphysics was empirically based, Teilhard overstated his case and invited sharp criticism from other natural scientists. Likewise, Teilhard's understanding of the role of human beings in cosmic evolution is much too anthropocentric, thus once again risking criticism or even ridicule from natural scientists.

Furthermore, his understanding of the Omega Point as focused on Christ as the Word Incarnate is, in my judgment, questionable from both a philosophical and theological perspective. Philosophically, Teilhard is confusing a key part of the whole, the person of Christ, with the whole of reality, the overarching unity of God with the world of creation both here and now, but above all at the end of the cosmic process, namely, "superlife" in an absolute sense. Theologically, Teilhard failed to see the pertinence of Aquinas's understanding of the doctrine of the Trinity, in particular his understanding of the divine Persons as "subsistent relations." In this way their individual identity as different divine Persons is one and the same with their corporate identity as One God.[37] Hence, it is a mistake, in my judgment, to focus on just one of the divine Persons, union with whom is the goal of the cosmic process.

In the next chapter my focus is on another twentieth-century philosopher-scientist, Alfred North Whitehead. Like Teilhard de Chardin, Whitehead saw the limitations of a purely objective approach to scientific method in discerning how evolution works within physical reality. But he set forth his explanation of how evolution proceeds in systematically defined terms rather than in the language of metaphor employed by Teilhard. Admittedly, his philosophical cosmology, just like that of

---

[37] Aquinas, *Summa theologiae* I, Q. 29, art. 4.

Teilhard, was largely neglected or openly dismissed as fanciful by both the proponents of classical metaphysics and by the great bulk of the scientific community. For Whitehead, like Teilhard, introduced subjectivity, the hidden potentiality for change and development, into the semi-mechanical workings of a purely objective and rationally ordered worldview. Thereby, he violated what is generally seen as one of the cardinal principles of careful thinking. Pure chance or unpredictability in any form, whether in the human mind or in the workings of nature, should be reduced to a minimum so as to guarantee the maximum amount of certainty in one's claims about the nature of reality. The bigger question, of course, is whether in the face of dramatically unexpected changes in human understanding of the world around oneself (for example, the alleged arrival of the Anthropocene era of the earth's history), one should instead start thinking "outside the box," imagining new and relatively untried alternatives to dealing with the reality of self, other human beings, the nonhuman natural world, and ultimately the transcendent reality of God.

Chapter 2

Whitehead's Philosophical Cosmology

Alfred North Whitehead was born in 1861 in Kent, England, the son of a recently ordained Anglican priest. After prep school in Dorchestershire he enrolled at Trinity College, Cambridge University. There he acquired first a BA, then an MA, and finally a DSc (Doctor of Science). He had a special interest in mathematics, and early in his academic career co-authored with Bertrand Russell the multi-volume *Principia Mathematica* that set forth the underlying mathematical principles in the workings of the natural world. In 1911 he began teaching at University College, London, as professor of applied mathematics. During that time he proposed an alternative explanation of Albert Einstein's theories of special and general relativity. In 1924 he received a five-year appointment to Harvard University. In his early years at Harvard he developed a new philosophical cosmology, initially in *Science and the Modern World* (1925), and then in *Process and Reality: An Essay in Cosmology* (1929). These two publications are the focus of my analysis of Whitehead's philosophy in this chapter.

Like Teilhard, Whitehead realized that early-modern natural science had unconsciously abstracted from the creativity and spontaneity at work in nature, given the focus on its standard mode of operation in terms of mathematically formulated laws and principles. There must be a way, likewise, to highlight the key role of subjectivity or spontaneity in bringing about evolutionary change and growth in the workings of physical reality.

Science
and the Modern World

In the opening pages of *Science and the Modern World*, for example, Whitehead says that there is an intrinsic order in the way that nature works, but paradoxically, "nothing ever really recurs in exact detail" (5).[1] No two days in the life of a human being, for example, are precisely alike. Hence, one has to attend to the empirical details of a given experience as well as look for universal laws and principles in its regular mode of operation. This is indeed fully in line with conventional scientific thinking. But in the search for universal principles many scientists overlook or ignore important details in the way that nature seems to work (21). Whitehead, for example, took note of what seemed to be a paradox in the quantum theory of his day. Electrons and other "primordial elements" of physical reality do not seem to exist continuously but to become manifest in scientific experiments now in one spatial location, now in another some distance away from the first location. Hence, electrons behave less like enduring mini-things and more like waves with "the vibratory ebb and flow of an underlying energy, or activity" (35). An electron is, then, in Whitehead's mind, a temporally recurrent energy-event rather than an enduring mini-thing at a given location. This leads him then to conclude that an electron is a mini-organism (what in *Process and Reality* he later calls an "actual entity" or "actual occasion," that is, a momentary self-constituting subject of

---

[1] Alfred North Whitehead, *Science and the Modern World* (New York: Free Press, 1967), 3. In what follows, the page number of the text of *Science and the Modern World* is provided in parentheses wherever needed.

experience).[2] It is as a result something alive, rather than a continuously existing, inert bit of matter, as most natural scientists of his day believed (36). But then a new philosophical question arises. Is physical reality as a result constituted by an ongoing series of events with a persistent pattern of existence and activity (what Whitehead calls societies and I refer to as systems), or is it still constituted by Aristotelian substances, that is, individual things that basically stay the same from moment to moment with only "accidental" modifications as a result of interactions with other substances or individual things? Common-sense experience favors the second alternative, but, as Whitehead notes above, scientific research at the atomic and molecular levels of existence and activity seems to point in the direction of the second alternative. Whitehead's purpose in writing first *Science and the Modern World* and then *Process and Reality* is to demonstrate that the second alternative is indeed the better way to proceed in coming to understand the dynamic character of physical reality.

Critique of Assumptions of Early Modern Science

Whitehead notes, for example, that in the 1700s the scientific understanding of physical reality was dominated by fixed principles of being that one learned by a process of induction and careful observation of things as they happen (41). But induction, says Whitehead, is a risky way to prove the universal validity of a hypothesis. One instance to the contrary disproves the universality of the induction. For example, noting the existence of one black swan disproves the claim that all swans are white. Rather, in Whitehead's view, the key to success in scientific research is not to be found in observing

---

[2] Alfred North Whitehead, *Process and Reality: An Essay in Cosmology*, corrected ed., ed. David Ray Griffin and Donald W. Sherburne (New York: Free Press, 1978), 18. N.B.: A momentary subject of experience is an event because it is in that single moment becoming something alive with an internal principle of activity (an organism as opposed to an abstract object of thought).

the world of nature "from the outside," so to speak, that is, as an external observer. Rather, the key to understanding the workings of nature is to be found instead in observing reality "from the inside," that is, by reflecting on the workings of one's own mind. For, upon introspection, one recognizes that every successive moment in one's consciousness is a new event, but also that it is heavily conditioned by what happened just a moment ago and by what is likely to happen in the next moment of consciousness (44). But if this is the way the human mind works, why not further conclude that this is also the way that everything else in the world works? That is, everything that exists here and now has a history behind it and a future in front of it. From moment to moment everything in this world is involved in an ongoing process of becoming something other than what it is right now. A washing machine, admittedly, can be said to be the same thing from moment to moment, but its real value lies in what it does from moment to moment as an ongoing process. Clothes are first automatically washed with soap, then rinsed and semi-dried before being transferred to the dryer, itself another process, to make the clothes ready for use again. Looked at casually, washers and dryers are machines, unchanging or fixed things. But their value lies in what they do, not what they are in themselves. For they are soon discarded and replaced by other machines if they do not work properly.

The process-oriented approach to reality is even more evident when one reflects on the inner workings of organisms. A human being, for example, is an ongoing life-process: one is born, lives for a certain amount of time, gradually declines in virility and eventually dies. Accordingly, while in common-sense experience the world would seem to be constituted by fixed or unchanging things located in space and time, upon closer inspection the things in this world are one and all processes, that is, organized systems of dynamically interrelated events with a given pattern or relatively fixed mode of operation in their ever-changing relations to one another.

The classical concepts of substance and accident are then somewhat deceptive because they abstract from the particularity of individual entities to focus on what they have in common as a group or given type of entity.[3] But any given entity is much more than simply an Aristotelian substance, a relatively fixed reality existing in its own right independent of other entities past and present. On closer examination it is in subtle ways always changing. Hence, it really is not an unchanging thing but instead a process or series of events that follow a consistent pattern or mode of operation. Moreover, since it is a natural process, it is likewise an organism, something that exists because of continuous interaction among its constituent parts or members. A mountain, for example, may seem to be a strictly inanimate thing that never changes. But geologists tell us that mountains undergo subtle changes in shape and size with the passage of time. Their ultimate components, atoms and molecules, are constantly in motion. Ever so slowly these atoms and molecules are changing their previous mode of interaction in response to various environmental factors. Plants, animals, and human beings, of course, are much more obviously organisms since they are internally organized in terms of having a "soul," or higher-order principle of operation, that entities like mountains and other strictly inanimate things do not possess. In brief, then, the world of nature is not dead but alive, that is, capable of spontaneous growth and evolutionary development with the passage of time (54).

Space and Time as Organic Realities

Whitehead further illustrates what he means by a world full of organisms rather than inanimate things in setting forth his theory of space and time as organic realities, unities of dynamically interrelated parts or members. For space can be subdivided into separate spaces, and yet each sub-space is an integral part of space as a whole. So every sub-space is in itself

---

[3] See, for example, the discussion of the preference for universal concepts in the philosophy and theology of the Middle Ages in the preceding chapter.

a unity of still smaller spaces and, in conjunction with other sub-spaces, makes up the reality of space as a whole. The same is true of time. Each duration or time-interval is a reality in its own right and yet only makes sense in terms of its relation to past and future moments of time, and thus to time as a whole (64–65).

Whitehead also notes that for one of his predecessors in the history of English philosophy, Bishop George Berkeley, "mind is the only absolute reality, and the unity of nature is the unity of ideas in the mind of God" (68). But this means that the mind of God is likewise an organism, a dynamic unity of interrelated parts or members. Whitehead further claims that, if the mind of God is an organism, then God necessarily views the world from God's own subjective perspective. The world, in other words, provides the data for God's own subjective life. Similarly, every moment in human consciousness is an organic unity that sees itself and the world around it from its own subjective perspective (69–70). But then, why not say that every physical entity in this world experiences every other entity around it organically, that is, from its own subjective perspective? Thus everything in this world has meaning and value to the extent that it is itself an organic unity and contributes to organic realities bigger than itself. The world is therefore alive, not dead, because it is an organic reality, not a cosmic machine.

Whitehead finds confirmation for his organismic understanding of reality by citing at some length the poetry of Milton, Pope, Wordsworth, and Tennyson. They too envisioned the world of nature as an organic reality, with emphasis on the value of each individual entity as a microcosm of the entire world around it. Moreover, natural scientists are also increasingly viewing the world of nature as at least a unified whole, if not always as an organism. For example, natural scientists have come to see that space is not empty but rather is filled with entities in dynamic interaction (98). Space, in other words, is not simply a theoretical concept in geometry, but a physical field of activity for entities in dynamic interrelation. The entities within the field do not remain the same but evolve in their basic structure and mode of operation with the passage of time (102). Yet, if this is the case, natural scientists are always in some fashion dealing with changing organic realities in their scientific research. Physics and chemistry are the study of smaller organisms (atoms and molecules); biology is the study of bigger organisms (cells as body parts). Hence, from still another point of view, nature is not constituted by inanimate things of various sizes and shapes but by different kinds of organisms (104–5). Whitehead calls this process-oriented or event-oriented approach to physical reality "organic mechanism" (106–7). That is, every event, large or small, is a mini-organism that affects every other event within the world of nature, which is itself an organic reality.

Critique of Twentieth-Century Natural Science

In the next two chapters of *Science and the Modern World* Whitehead compares his own organismic approach to physical reality with important new insights in twentieth-century science: Einstein's theory of special and general relativity; and quantum theory (research into the ultimate constituents of physical reality). In both cases he has a different explanation for what is going on in the world of nature than that provided by conventional natural science. Einstein, for example, claimed that all physical entities are constantly in motion, undergoing changes in their location in space and time. Entities that are changing their location in space and time at roughly the same speed seem to be at rest vis-à-vis one another. Entities that are changing their location in space and time at different speeds or velocities do not share the same space-time dimensions. For entities traveling at high speeds, a single moment of time (for example, a second or a minute) lasts longer, and the distance traveled from one moment to another increases. For entities traveling at lower speeds, a single moment of time passes more quickly and the distance traveled from one moment to another shrinks (122). Whitehead, on the contrary, claims that every process (ordered sequence of events) generates its own sense of space and time in accord with the pace of its own process of becoming. As a result, mosquitos with an average lifespan of less than two months experience space and time differently than human beings, whose average lifespan is measured in years, not days or months. So, whereas Einstein claimed that space-time as an objective reality is altered by the speed at which entities are moving through it, Whitehead claims that the time and space parameters within an organism are relative to its pace of change vis-à-vis other organisms in their own process of self-constitution. The empirical measurement of space and time is the same in the theories of Einstein and Whitehead, but the two differ dramatically in their metaphysical presuppositions about the nature of reality. Einstein believed that the ultimate units of reality are unchanging inanimate things; Whitehead claimed that the ultimate units of reality are ever-changing events or mini-organisms.

With reference to quantum mechanics Whitehead once again has a different explanation of what is really going on than Einstein and other physicists. In their view a photon or light wave from the sun moves progressively through space and time with a persistent, vibratory motion, rising and falling over and over again (like a wave of water moving to the shore), until it comes to its destination and discharges its quota of energy upon the body of a human being or some other form of plant and animal life on earth. Thus the light wave continuously exists as one and the same entity as it moves through space and time (133). For Whitehead, on the contrary, a light wave is an organism that comes into existence and goes out of existence from one moment to the next in its movement through space and time. Thus, the path of a photon through space and time is a series of overlapping events, not the trajectory of a continuously existing material entity as would be expected in classical physics (135). Whitehead thus has a plausible explanation for the otherwise baffling indeterminacy in the mode of operation of photons and other subatomic particles within quantum theory. The indeterminacy arises from the fact that successive events, unlike inanimate things, do not continuously exist but appear and disappear, becoming something new and slightly different at each new location in space and moment of time. A photon, accordingly, does not travel at the speed of 186,000 miles per second (as Einstein believed) but changes location in space and time at the same speed of 186,000 miles per second. The mathematical results in both theories for the speed of light are the same, but the metaphysical presuppositions are totally different.

Subjectivity and Objectivity

Whitehead then calls attention in *Science and the Modern World* to the uneasy relation between philosophy and science in the modern era. Contemporary philosophy and theology have become "tinged with subjectivism" as opposed to the ideal of objectivity in the natural sciences (140). For example, Descartes made individual subjective experience (*cogito, ergo sum*) the starting point for reflection on the God-world relationship, and Locke focused on the internal workings of the human mind in the act of cognition. Natural science, however, continues to pursue the goal of objective certitude about enduring relations between inanimate entities. The result is that philosophy and religion in the modern era have had little or no effective impact on the scientific understanding of the natural world (142). But Whitehead then qualifies that assumption by singling out the work of philosopher-psychologist William James, especially his contention that the human mind is not a nonmaterial entity separate from the body, but rather a higher-order function of the brain as a physical organism (143–44). Thus, human cognition is the mind's ongoing experience of itself as a working physical organism rather than as an unchanging nonmaterial reality (148–49). Mind and matter are not independent realities with little or no connection to one another, but dynamically interrelated processes as in an organic understanding of physical reality (152). Yet not everything in this world is in constant flux. Whitehead allows for the existence and activity of "eternal objects" in the ongoing self-constitution of organisms. Eternal objects are, for Whitehead, like universal concepts or intelligible forms in classical metaphysics in that they are abstractions from the concrete particularity of individual material entities (159). They do not exist in their own right but only as active in the workings of individual organisms. At the same time, these eternal objects are internally related to one another (for example, the color blue as opposed to the colors yellow, red, green, and so forth). Related to one another in this way, eternal objects co-constitute a single unified realm of dynamically interrelated "relational essences" (160). Taken together, they thus represent the world of abstract possibility as opposed to the world of concrete actuality.

But where specifically is this all-encompassing realm of eternal objects to be found? Here Whitehead introduces his notion of God as the principle of concretion (174); that is, the eternal objects exist in the first place in the mind of God who offers a specific set of eternal objects to each physical organism to help it in its process of self-constitution. Human beings and other sentient creatures, of course, are still responsible for whatever self-constituting decision they finally make. But God's antecedent ordering of eternal objects as intelligible possibilities is very valuable for making a good choice rather than a bad choice. Yet something else is needed for the self-constitution of a physical organism at every moment, namely, the energy actually to make a self-constituting decision to be this kind of entity rather than that. This energy, says Whitehead, does not come from God but from the inbuilt creativity of the evolutionary process itself. For otherwise God would be held responsible for all the evil in the world that happens as a result of bad choices on the part of creatures in successive moments of experience (179). Rather, God's role in the cosmic process is simply "to divide the Good from the Evil, and to establish Reason 'within her dominions supreme'" (179). In this way Whitehead cleverly dodges the classic problem of theodicy, namely, how to justify the reality of physical and moral evil in a world created by an all-loving God.

Science and Religion in Dialogue

In the concluding chapters of *Science and the Modern World* Whitehead offers a suggestion for the future of the dialogue between religion and science. He notes that, while religion and science are "the two strongest general forces" that influence the lives of human beings (181), their respective truth-claims often conflict because of half-truths made in their defense by both sides. An apparent contradiction in rival truth-claims, however, should be treated as a challenge to achieve an even better understanding of the true relation of religion and science to one another. If religion currently seems to be more on the defensive than science, it can regain its old power over the minds and hearts of human beings if it "can face change in the same spirit as science" (189). That is, theologians should recognize that while the basic teachings of their religion may be eternally true, the way to understand and to express those principles is time-bound, heavily conditioned by "the imaginative picture of the world expressed in previous ages" (189). Put in the context of a new worldview, these same teachings will instead acquire new relevance for the faithful. Likewise, Whitehead urges both natural scientists and theologians to work with his governing presupposition in *Science and the Modern World* that matter is not dead, but alive, endowed with subjectivity and/or spontaneity as its internal principle of organization, in the same way the human mind functions but to a lesser degree (194–96). For a focus on mind alone, to the virtual exclusion of the embodiment of mind in matter (195–96), leads to a dangerous spirit of individualism, a loss of a sense of community with other human beings and the natural world. But a focus on matter to the virtual exclusion of spirit leads to "a lack of reverence in the treatment of natural and artistic beauty" (196). That is, over-specialization in scientific research leads to a shrunken understanding of what life is all about and how the world actually works. Nature is not a cosmic machine but a cosmic organism. Individual entities have value to the extent that they contribute to an organic value greater than themselves as individuals: "A forest is the triumph of the organization of mutually dependent species" (206). Individual trees, plants, and animal species exist for the sake of the forest, and yet the forest only exists because of the ongoing interdependence of the various forms of life within it.

I now turn to a summary and analysis of Whitehead's most important book: *Process and Reality: An Essay in Cosmology*. Whereas in *Science and the Modern World* he offered a critique of the implicit metaphysical presuppositions of early modern natural science, in *Process and Reality* he systematically sets forth his own worldview or philosophical cosmology. References to other scientists and philosophers with their different points of view are incidental to the detailed presentation of his own philosophical scheme. As a result, in the second part of this chapter I am more selective in my summary and analysis of the contents of the book.[4]

Process and Reality

Whitehead initially notes his connection with the tradition of British Empiricism, especially with the philosophy of John Locke. Locke focused on the way that human beings perceive reality all around them from moment to moment (xi). Whitehead's basic hypothesis in *Process and Reality* is quite similar, namely, that the best clue to the workings of physical reality everywhere is to be found in careful observation and analysis of the workings of one's own mental experience—in particular, the succession of events that make up human self-awareness from moment to moment. That said, Whitehead then lays out the requirements of any speculative philosophy, his own work included. "The philosophical scheme should be coherent, logical, and, in respect to its interpretation, applicable and

---

[4] In the following the page number of the text of *Process and Reality* is provided in parentheses wherever needed.

adequate" (3). That is, a cosmology or worldview should be internally well organized and externally applicable to all the facts of human experience, not just some of the facts. At the same time, Whitehead does not claim that his or anyone else's philosophical scheme is universally valid: "Words and phrases must be stretched towards a generality foreign to their ordinary usage; and however much elements of language be stabilized as technicalities, they remain metaphors mutely appealing for an imaginative leap" (4). Hence, a philosophical cosmology is akin to a scientific hypothesis. That is, if a hypothesis seems to correlate well with the data of sense experience, then it should be accepted as provisionally true, but only until and unless new empirical evidence or a better explanatory theory becomes available to warrant setting it aside as either mistaken or only partially true.

Creativity as Ultimate Reality

Whitehead then clarifies what he means by a key term in his own cosmology: *creativity*. In *Science and the Modern World* he distinguishes between creativity as the underlying energy source for the cosmic process and God as the Principle of Concretion or limitation for all the possibilities available to human beings and other sentient creatures in their use of creativity for making decisions from moment to moment. Here, at the start of *Process and Reality*, he makes a much bolder claim: creativity is Ultimate Reality in virtue of which everything exists (7). God too exists in virtue of creativity. What then is creativity, such that even God needs creativity to exist, to be God? "It is that ultimate principle by which the many, which are the universe disjunctively, become the one actual occasion, which is the universe conjunctively" (21). That is, in virtue of creativity, God from moment to moment unifies everything that just happened in the world within the unity of God's own conscious experience of the world here and now. Similarly, human beings and other sentient creatures use creativity to unify the sense data coming from their perception of the world around them into the unity of their experience of the world from moment to moment.

Creativity then is Ultimate Reality, but only as an underlying activity, not as an entity in its own right. As such, it is the underlying energy source for everything that from moment to moment comes into existence. Whitehead calls these creative moments *actual occasions* or *actual entities*. For they last only a moment and are replaced by a successor event in the same series of ongoing events. Whitehead calls them actual occasions or actual entities because they are active subjects of experience rather than inert material entities. In their brief moment of existence they become themselves and establish their identity in relation to everything and everyone else currently existing. They are then strictly relational entities that only exist in terms of their dynamic relation to other entities. Likewise, they are time-bound entities as well as spatially extended entities. That is, they not only have a sense of location in space but also a sense of past and future as well as a sense of the present moment. They in some measure repeat the past and anticipate the future in their brief moment of self-constitution.

This understanding of the nature of reality in terms of a succession of momentary subjects of experience, no doubt, seems bizarre to many people because they habitually live in the world of common-sense experience, a world made up of all kinds of individual entities with little or no intrinsic relation to one another. Moreover, this common-sense point of view nicely corresponds to the metaphysics of being that Aquinas and other medieval philosophers and theologians worked out to explain the Christian God-world relationship. God is the Supreme Being or topmost entity in a hierarchically ordered world of lesser entities. Whitehead, however, in focusing on a world constituted by successive events, not enduring things, is setting up a new metaphysics of becoming: a world made up of processes, large and small, complex or relatively simple, all existing from moment to moment in virtue of creativity as the principle of novelty within the cosmic process (21). Accordingly, everyone and everything (even God) is in some modest way not the same, but new from moment to moment. Furthermore, because both God and finite entities are in ongoing evolution or change vis-à-vis one another, the cosmic process has no beginning or end.

Here Whitehead is closer in spirit to Aristotle than to Aquinas and the classical tradition. That is, for Aristotle the cosmic process had no beginning and no end because its first principle, the Unmoved Mover, was really not a fixed entity but an unceasing activity, "thought thinking itself" over and over again.[5] Aquinas, however, replaced Aristotle's understanding of the Unmoved Mover with the biblical understanding of God as Creator of heaven and earth. God is then outside of and basically transcendent of the world or cosmic process. Accordingly, the world had a beginning and will have an end because God is its First Cause, its transcendent Creator, and its Final End.[6] Whitehead's metaphysics of becoming, however, has no beginning or end: "God and the world are the contrasted opposites in terms of which Creativity [as a transcendent activity] achieves its supreme task of transforming disjoined multiplicity, with its diversities in opposition, into concrescent unity, with its diversities in contrast" (348). So both God and the world (some world, even if not this particular world) forever coexist as the conjoint terms of the unending creative activity of turning multiplicity into unity.

Entities as Structured Societies

Stability within Whitehead's metaphysics of becoming is guaranteed by what Whitehead calls *societies,* sets of successive actual entities or momentary subjects of experience with a "common element of form" or "defining characteristic" (34). This "common element of form" is somewhat akin to what

---

[5] W. T. Jones, *A History of Western Philosophy,* vol. 1, *The Classical Mind,* 2nd ed. (New York: Harcourt, Brace, and World, 1952), 228–32.

[6] Thomas Aquinas, *Summa theologiae* I, Q. 2, art. 3.

Aquinas and other classical metaphysicians characterized as the substantial form of a physical entity, that which gives the entity a sense of permanence and stability. But within classical metaphysics, the substantial form of a physical entity exercises agency, that is, is active in giving form or shape to the material constituents of the entity. Within a Whiteheadian society, however, it is the constituents (momentary self-constituting subjects of experience) that exercise agency vis-à-vis one another so as to first generate and then perpetuate in time and space this "common element of form" or "defining characteristic" of the society. Hence, the governing structure of a Whiteheadian society has no subjective agency in its own right. It is the ongoing result or byproduct of the interaction between its constituent actual entities or actual occasions. Thus, Whitehead's metaphysics of becoming focuses on evolution, ongoing orderly change from "the bottom up." Aquinas's metaphysics of being focuses on a relatively unchanging world in which continuity is guaranteed in each instance by reason of the "top down" activity of an unchanging substantial form in dealing with its material constituents.

But is a Whiteheadian society then simply the sum of its parts, its constituent actual entities? Or is it an objective reality in itself, something more than the sum of its parts? Whitehead claims that a society is self-sustaining; it is its own reason for existence (89). Thus, it is a reality in its own right (like an Aristotelian substance). Hence, it is not simply the sum of its constituent parts at any given moment. But at the same time, "there is no society in isolation" (90). Every society exists within a social context, an even broader "society" of actual entities of which it is a constituent member or sub-society. In addition, there is ongoing interaction between the more comprehensive society and all its sub-societies. That is, each sub-society has to work within the objective parameters set by the mode of operation of the bigger society, and the bigger society itself only works well if it integrates the workings of the sub-societies into its own mode of operation.

There is, in other words, a reciprocal causality constantly at work between the larger society and all its sub-societies and between the sub-societies in their ongoing relation to one another.

This understanding of Whiteheadian societies may seem overly complicated to many people. But Whitehead is trying to explain evolution both within oneself and in the world at large. Evolution, however, works simultaneously "from the bottom up" and "from the top down." The agents of evolutionary change within an organism are its constituent parts (actual entities). But they are limited or constrained in their interaction by the current structure or mode of operation of the organism as a whole. Whitehead further explains this reciprocal relation between the parts and the whole in the following citation from *Process and Reality:* "The society is only efficient through its individual members [its constituent actual entities]," and yet "the members can only exist by reason of the laws which dominate the society" (91). The governing structure or mode of operation of the organism thus exercises top-down causation in the way that it limits the activity of its constituent actual entities every moment. But, unlike a substantial form in classical metaphysics, it is not as a result a subjective agent exercising efficient causality and thereby actively giving order and intelligibility to its relatively passive constituent parts or members. It is simply an objective structure that limits or constrains the range of activity for its constituent actual entities from moment to moment. Hence, causality within an organism is reciprocal, not unilateral, as is the case in classical metaphysics with its accepted understanding of the relation between matter and form. Furthermore, interaction among societies, as noted above, is also reciprocal. For, when societies engage with one another, they create a common field of activity for their interaction. Within that higher-order common field of activity the constituent actual entities of individual sub-societies have contact with one another and thus through reciprocal causation influence one another's self-constitution.

Growth in Size and Complexity

Given this understanding of the workings of societies, Whitehead then sketches the historical development of our "cosmic
epoch" (96–97). With the expression "cosmic epoch," of course,
he allows for the possibility that the present world is just one
of a series of epochs in the overall history of the universe. Each
of these epochs has characteristics not shared with the other
epochs. Our epoch began with what Whitehead calls a "geometrical society," a network of abstract geometrical shapes and
sizes that laid the groundwork for future actual entities in their
geometrical relations to one another. The initial constituents of
these geometrical societies were "electromagnetic occasions,"
momentary self-constituting subjects of experience that were
dynamically interrelated in terms of different geometrical patterns. Over time these electromagnetically charged subjects of
experience aggregated into relatively simple societies, and then
into ever more complex "structured societies," that is, societies
composed of sub-societies, once again each with its own set
of constituent actual entities (99). Thus ever more complex
societies of actual entities came into existence: "regular trains
of brain waves, individual electrons, protons, individual molecules, societies of molecules such as inorganic bodies, living
cells, and societies of cells such as vegetable and animal bodies" (98).

Whitehead distinguishes here between societies of actual entities that constitute inanimate entities (for example,
human-made artifacts like tables and chairs; or artifacts of
nature like rocks, minerals, metals, and so on) and societies
of actual entities that constitute living entities (plant and animal bodies). With reference to inanimate entities, Whitehead
claims that they are composed of actual entities that have no
internal principle of organization over and above their dynamic interrelation with one another at each moment (99). In
this sense they are a democracy because the actual occasions
have more or less equal influence on one another's individual
self-constitution. But for the same reason this kind of society

appears to be lifeless; there is little or no perceptible change in its external mode of operation. But as contemporary research in physics and chemistry makes clear, there is a great deal of unseen activity at the atomic and molecular level of existence for these allegedly inanimate entities. Even sturdily constructed inanimate things wear out or break apart, partly because of external forces of nature like weather, temperature, and so on, but also partly because their component atoms and molecules no longer work together smoothly in response to those external forces of nature. So, all appearances to the contrary, these inanimate things are still in a minimal sense "alive"; that is, their component atoms and molecules are alert to and responsive to one another and to their physical environment.

Beginning with cells, however, life and spontaneity become empirically observable. The cell is no longer a democracy in the organization of its constituent actual entities/self-constituting subjects of experience but rather a monarchy. That is, one subset of actual entities becomes "regnant" over the other subsets of actual entities within what Whitehead calls a "structured society," a society composed of sub-societies of actual entities, all of them functioning together as an organic whole (103). That is, the common element of form or governing structure of the regnant subset of actual entities has a strong but somewhat indirect influence on the self-constitution of the constituent actual entities in all the other subsets of actual entities. It serves as the internal principle of self-organization for all of them together as a very simple life-form. What in classical metaphysics is called a vegetative soul, performs this same function in various forms of plant life.[7] There is a significant difference, however, between Whitehead's understanding of the governing structure of a regnant subset of actual entities within a structured society and the notion of an animal soul or a rational soul in a human being within classical metaphysics. For Whitehead, the governing structure of the regnant subset of actual entities within a "structured society" is emergent out of

---

[7] Ibid., I, Q. 78, art. 1.

the ongoing synthesis or byproduct of the interrelated activity of all its constituent actual entities. But for classical thinkers like Aquinas, the "sensitive" soul of an animal or the rational soul of a human being is a nonmaterial entity, a substantial form introduced by God into material components so as to constitute a new body-soul unity.[8] For Aquinas, accordingly, the substantial form with its nonmaterial agency governs the material constituents; for Whitehead, the collective agency of the constituent actual entities instead determines the "common element of form" or governing structure of the structured society as a whole. For example, in his explanation of the reciprocal relation between the mind or brain and the body in human beings, Whitehead first notes that most of the actual entities in the human body do not possess as much spontaneity or originality in their self-constitution as do the actual entities in the top-most or regnant subset of actual entities in the human mind (103). Most of them simply pass on to their successor actual entities the same "common element of form" or basic pattern of organization as they themselves possess. The actual entities/subjects of experience in the regnant subset of actual entities or "soul," on the contrary, are much more contingent in the way that they interact with one another. Thus, these actual entities can change the mode of operation of the structured society as a whole (the body-soul unity) in an unexpected direction, that is, either toward further growth and development or toward progressive decline and the eventual death of the organism (103). Whereas a higher-order animal (such as a cat or dog) has the beginnings of a "personality" (107), the human being has the full flowering of a "personality" able to make conscious decisions and be responsible to others for those same decisions (108). For Whitehead, then, personality is emergent out of the reciprocal relation between the mind and the body. For Aquinas, personality is derivative from the workings of a nonmaterial soul introduced into the body by God at the moment of conception or some time thereafter.

---

[8] Ibid., I, Q. 75, art. 1.

Cosmic Process as Ultimate Reality

As remarked earlier in this chapter, Whitehead is closer to Aristotle than to Aquinas in his understanding of the God-world relationship. For him, as for Aristotle, the cosmic process, rather than God or the Unmoved Mover, is Ultimate Reality. That is, for both Aristotle and Whitehead, God and the Unmoved Mover are constituents of the cosmic process, not transcendent of it. For example, in the last chapter of *Process and Reality* Whitehead says: "God and the World are the contrasted opposites in terms of which Creativity achieves its supreme task of transforming disjoined multiplicity, with its diversities in opposition, into concrescent unity, with its diversities in contrast" (348). Creativity, then, as the underlying principle of the cosmic process whereby the "Many" become "One" and then are increased by one over and over again (21), is Ultimate Reality because it empowers the existence and activity of both God and the world. That is, God serves as the transcendent principle of the One, and the world serves as the ongoing principle of the many. Creativity keeps God and the world in this dynamic interrelationship at every moment. But it is not in itself a higher-order entity but a higher-order activity. It is thus the key component in a metaphysics of becoming but not in a metaphysics of being. In a metaphysics of being, a higher-order entity (for example, God as Creator of heaven and earth) is Ultimate Reality.

Yet, simply as the ongoing principle of the One vis-à-vis the World as the ongoing principle of the many, God still plays an indispensable role in Whitehead's philosophical cosmology. God "saves" the world by giving it enduring meaning and value in what would otherwise be a meaningless succession of purely transient events. For God has two natures or constitutive components. In God's "primordial nature," God is the unlimited conceptual realization of the absolute wealth of potentiality" (343). Hence, in virtue of his primordial nature, God can provide initial subjective aims (feeling-level urges) to finite actual entities to choose something good and worthwhile in their individual processes of self-constitution (245). The individual actual entity is indeed free to accept or reject (at least in part) this feeling-level urge to a higher-order value by God. It may instead yield to feeling-level urges from its own past history that are much more narrowly defined and self-centered. Yet in and through the divine primordial nature God exercises a providential care for what happens within the cosmic process from moment to moment. God is continually at work to keep the cosmic process "on the right track."

Likewise, in God's "consequent nature," God unifies within God's own subjective experience of the world everything that just happened, thereby restoring order and directionality to the cosmic process even with all the widely divergent decisions made by finite actual entities a moment ago (345). Whitehead adds, in a more interpersonal vein:

> The results of destructive evil, purely self-regarding, are dismissed into their triviality of merely individual facts; and yet the good that they did achieve in individual joy, in individual sorrow, in the introduction of needed contrast, is yet saved by its relation to the completed whole. The image—and it is but an image—the image under which this operative growth of God's nature is best conceived, is that of a tender care that nothing be lost. (346)

So Whitehead, a rationally inclined philosopher of science, provides here at the end of *Process and Reality* an overall understanding of the cosmic process that closely resembles what Christians call salvation, based on their reading of the Bible. What is missing in Whitehead's understanding of salvation is any reference to subjective immortality for human beings, the possibility of life after death. That is, all human beings and indeed all of creation find de facto objective immortality through their incorporation into the ongoing consequent nature of God as noted above. But as a philosopher rather than a theologian, Whitehead prefers only to hint at the possibility of subjective immortality for human beings and indeed for the cosmic process as a whole in the following ambiguous statement: "In everlastingness, immediacy is reconciled with objective immortality" (351). But what is meant here by the term *immediacy*? Does this imply subjective immortality for the creature within "everlastingness" (the divine consequent nature) upon cessation of existence in this world? Whitehead is silent on that point.

Critique and Evaluation

By way of a brief critique of Whitehead's cosmology, I note in the first place his claim that, if the cosmic process is to have intrinsic meaning and value over and above a random succession of events, then the fundamental components of physical reality cannot be inert bits of matter that are pushed and pulled in different directions by chance, simply as a result of external environmental influences (for example, gravity and electromagnetism). These "primordial elements" must instead possess some minimal form of subjectivity whereby they can on a feeling-level both be aware of and respond to persistent patterns occurring in the world around them. Inert things, on the contrary, are incapable of any such minimal self-awareness. They possess no internal potentiality to be anything other than what they are right now. So both Whitehead and, as already noted, Teilhard de Chardin are in my view to be commended for their farsighted quite remarkable insights into the deeper workings of physical reality. But, whereas Teilhard grounded his basic insight into subjectivity as the necessary presupposition for evolution within the cosmic process in the language of metaphor (for example, the "inside" and the "outside" of things), Whitehead set forth his insight into subjectivity as the basis for evolution within the cosmic process in terms of a complex system of logically ordered concepts. Thereby, Whitehead's philosophical cosmology offered a much greater challenge to the purely materialistic presuppositions of the natural science of his day than did Teilhard, whose thought could be more readily dismissed by other natural scientists as appropriate for work in theology but of no use in natural science.

But Whitehead missed a key point that Teilhard consciously integrated into his understanding of the God-world relationship in *The Human Phenomenon,* namely, that subjectivity only makes complete sense in terms of intersubjectivity or shared existence. Admittedly, one's instinctive relation to things is to manipulate them in terms of one's antecedent interests and desires. But in relating to human beings and within limits to nonhuman subjects of experience, one finds oneself immediately engaged in receiving and responding to "signs" from those other subjects of experience. Martin Buber was perhaps the first major philosopher in the modern era to call attention to this basic difference between intersubjective I-Thou relations and purely impersonal I-It relations in human life.[9] To his credit, Teilhard came to the same conclusion as Buber in seeing this difference between I-Thou and I-It relations in human life. But, unlike Buber, he intuitively extended this principle of intersubjectivity into the workings of the world at large; thereby he made it the basis of his own evolutionary worldview. For, as noted earlier in Chapter 1, for Teilhard every entity, however minuscule, has both an "inside" and an "outside" and thus is both a subjective as well as an objective reality. Furthermore, the transcendent goal of the cosmic process is Omega Point in which the Cosmic Christ is the unifying center of the noosphere, itself an all-embracing system of dynamically interrelated finite centers of consciousness.

Whitehead, with his notion of society as the ongoing synthesis of the dynamic interrelation of momentary subjects of experience, could likewise have endorsed the notion of intersubjectivity as a foundational concept in his philosophical cosmology. But what presumably stood in the way was his antecedent commitment to philosophical atomism, that is, the

---

[9] Martin Buber, *I and Thou*, trans. Walter Kaufmann (New York: Scribner's, 1970), 62: "I require a You [Thou] to become; becoming I, I say You."

belief that in the end only individual entities exist, each reflecting the reality of the world around itself in a unique way.[10] Admittedly, in terms of the natural science of his day Whitehead was on safe ground in claiming that "contemporary events happen in *causal* independence of each other" (61). It takes time, for example, for sound waves to move from your lips to my ears. But with a little more imagination Whitehead could still have allowed for intersubjective relations between simultaneously existing societies in virtue of the ongoing interplay of their constituent actual entities with one another. Likewise, he failed to see that societies have an objective reality different from their constituent actual entities. If he had conceded that point, he might have reformulated his foundational principle in *Process and Reality:* the "final real things of which the world is made up" (18) are not simply actual entities that come and go with extreme rapidity, but likewise societies of actual entities that operate with an enduring "common element of form" (34). I will develop this idea at greater length in the next chapter.

---

[10] Whitehead, *Process and Reality,* 35, 22–23.

Chapter 3

A Systems-Oriented Approach to the God-World Relationship

In this chapter I combine insights from Teilhard de Chardin and from Alfred North Whitehead to sketch my own philosophical cosmology, so that in Chapter 4 I can use it as background for my vision of active (or, better said, interactive) church life in the twenty-first century. From Whitehead I borrow the notion that the "final real things of which the world is made up" are momentary mini-organisms (what Whitehead calls actual entities or actual occasions so as to emphasize their event-like occurrence), not enduring mini-things (atoms and molecules as conventionally understood in the natural sciences). From Teilhard de Chardin, I borrow what he calls the law of complexification-consciousness to describe the workings of cosmic evolution. I concur with him in supporting the idea of noogenesis, ongoing growth in collective cosmic consciousness, as the ultimate goal of the cosmic process. Where I differ from both Whitehead and Teilhard is in my more persistent affirmation that physical reality is socially constituted. That is, the value of the existence and activity of an individual entity is not to be found so much in the entity itself as in the way that it actively contributes to a socially organized reality greater than itself. This is not to deny the inviolable rights of human beings as individuals, but only to situate those rights in an inclusive rather than exclusive context, that is, with due reference to the rights of other human beings and to the common good (both human and nonhuman).

Thus, in opposition to Whitehead's preoccupation with the interplay of actual entities with one another, I emphasize instead the synthesis or objective result of this ongoing interaction between individual actual entities, namely, their self-organization into societies as socially organized realities in their own right. Likewise, I disagree with Teilhard's claim that the cosmic process will culminate in a "personalizing universe," an individual personal entity, namely, the Cosmic Christ. Rather, the culmination of cosmic noogenesis should be a transcendent collective reality. From a Christian perspective this would be the mystical body of Christ, with Christ himself as its head and primordial individual member. Teilhard himself seems to implicitly acknowledge that point when in *The Human Phenomenon* he claims that the Omega Point "can only be a distinct Center radiating at the core of a system of centers."[1] Yet this transcendent "Center" at the core of a system of centers is still itself a member of the system, albeit the key participant in the system. In addition, Teilhard failed to take into account that the Cosmic Christ is himself a participant in the more comprehensive divine Life-system, the eternally existent community of the three divine Persons. Hence, Teilhard, in my judgment, should have envisioned the Omega Point as the incorporation of the entire world of creation into the Trinity as an all-encompassing divine Life-system.

In what follows, then, I first set forth my own systems-oriented approach to reality, showing how it differs from Whitehead's explanation of the way that societies of dynamically interrelated actual entities function within the cosmic process. Then I indicate how my systems-oriented approach to reality

---

[1] Pierre Teilhard de Chardin, *The Human Phenomenon*, trans. Sarah Appleton-Weber (Brighton, OR: Sussex Academic Press, 1999), 186.

explains cosmic evolution—the emergence of plant and animal life and then of mind or self-awareness in human life—better than natural scientists like Stuart Kauffman, Terrence Deacon, and Jesper Hoffmeyer. Finally, in the third part of the chapter, I indicate how my systems-oriented approach to the God-world relationship provides a better explanation of orthodox Christian belief in the Trinity, the incarnation, and life after death than many other schemes put forward by contemporary systematic theologians or philosophers of science.

Society or System?

The term *society* is used by Whitehead to describe ongoing networks of dynamically interrelated subjects of experience; I use the term *system* for the same purpose. As I see it, *society* (like *community*) implicitly puts emphasis on the individual constituent parts or members of a socially organized reality; *system,* on the contrary, seems to focus more on the independent objective reality of this network of dynamically interrelated subjects of experience. In considering the age-old question of whether the whole is the sum of its parts or more than the sum of its parts, I favor the second alternative for both theological and philosophical reasons. Theologically, the Christian doctrine of the Trinity seems to favor the whole over the parts, the corporate unity of God over the plurality of individual divine Persons. For, as I explain below, the divine Persons find their individual identity in existing for and with one another within a transcendent life-system or perpetually enduring common life. Philosophically, I contest Whitehead's restriction of creativity (the principle of self-organization within the cosmic process) to the self-constitution of actual entities. I myself propose that creativity must also be at work in the formation of societies if societies are to be the enduring and relatively unchanging constituents of a socially organized world. At one point in *Process and Reality* Whitehead describes his philosophical cosmology as a "philosophy of organism."[2] Hence, Whiteheadian societies should likewise be organic realities on the corporate level of existence and activity within nature. That is, a Whiteadian society is not simply the sum of its parts (dynamically inter-related actual entities) at any given moment. It is a physical reality in its own right, an enduring unity of dynamically inter-related parts or members.[3]

But, if creativity is the internal principle of self-organization in physical reality whereby "the many become one and are increased by one,"[4] creativity should also logically be at work in the origination and growth of societies as well as in the self-constitution of its constituent individual actual entities from moment to moment. According to Whitehead, however, societies do not exercise any form of creativity. They are simply the ongoing byproduct of the interrelated activity of their constituent actual entities from moment to moment. Likewise, they do not exercise causal agency in their own right. The causal agency of a society in dealing with another society is dependent upon the interaction between the constituent actual entities of both societies upon one another within a common or shared field of activity. Hence, Whitehead felt justified in claiming that only actual entities exercise creativity.[5] But what Whitehead over-looked here was that every actual entity in the process of its individual self-constitution is at the same time co-constituting with other actual entities the objective corporate reality of the society to which they all belong. An individual actual entity, in other words, is a purely transient, basically incomplete reality if it simply lasts for a moment and then ceases to be. It derives its complete identity and enduring value not from itself but

---

[2] Alfred North Whitehead, *Process and Reality: An Essay in Cosmology*, corrected ed., ed. David Ray Griffin and Donald W. Sherburne (New York: Free Press, 1978), 7.

[3] Whitehead himself says as much in *Adventures of Ideas* (New York: Free Press, 1967), 204, a book published after *Process and Reality*.

[4] Whitehead, *Process and Reality*, 21.

[5] Ibid., 31.

from its active participation in sustaining the corporate reality of whatever society (or societies) to which it belongs.

Whitehead missed this further insight into the relationship between societies and their constituent actual entities presumably because he was conditioned by his previous training in mathematics and natural science to think of physical entities simply in terms of their constituent parts. One understands what something is and how it works if one can take it apart and put it back together again. But he may also have been unconsciously influenced by the traditional strong emphasis in Western civilization on the rights of human beings as individuals distinct from society at large. Be that as it may, Whitehead's key insight that actual entities (momentary self-constituting subjects of experience) are the primitive components or constitutive elements of physical reality is nevertheless invaluable in order to understand how life in all its varying forms emerged from the apparently inanimate workings of the cosmic process. As I make clear in the next section of this chapter, while most natural scientists are convinced of the objective reality of systems in the workings of the cosmic process, they have no philosophical explanation of how these systems exhibit over time more and more self-organization and spontaneity.

Scientific Explanation of the Emergence of Progressively Higher-Order Systems

As mentioned in Chapter 1, the medieval worldview was challenged on a variety of fronts in the sixteenth and seventeenth centuries in Western Europe. These included, for example, the conversion from a geocentric to a heliocentric understanding of the solar system in astronomy; the voyages of discovery to the non-Western world; the Protestant Reformation; and the philosophy of René Descartes, which postulated a radical difference between mind and matter. As a result, the traditional appeal to the Aristotelian four causes (material, formal, efficient, and final) for the explanation of the workings of physical reality was set aside in favor of the regular use of only two of these causes (material and efficient). Nature was viewed as matter in motion, with universal mathematical principles governing the way that material entities customarily are related to one another. The notion of immaterial forms as operational principles within physical entities and the sense of an inbuilt final causality or purposiveness in the mode of operation of those entities were thereby lost. Instead, physical reality was thought to be constituted by the ongoing interaction of inanimate atoms and molecules whose workings can be mathematically determined with a high degree of certitude.

Charles Darwin in his book *The Origin of Species* likewise carried forward this mechanistic approach to physical reality in his thinking about how natural selection among animal species worked.[6] He focused on a single impersonal principle, namely, that some organisms survive and others expire because they are better adapted to unexpected changes in the external environment than their contemporaries. But he did not move beyond the empirical data to explain how individual organisms acquired traits favorable to their survival and continued well-being and then passed them on to their progeny. Gregor Mendel, a nineteenth-century Augustinian friar and natural scientist, experimented with the interbreeding of yellow and green pea plants and discovered that some traits proper to these pea plants vary from one generation of pea plants to another. This insight into the way pea plants unexpectedly differ from one another eventually led to the notion of dominant and recessive genes and the new science of genetics at the beginning of the twentieth century. But genes, too, were initially understood and interpreted mechanistically; that is, genes were thought to be unchanging mini-entities that convey information (DNA) to the other constituents in a cell for the purposes of self-reproduction. Evelyn Fox Keller, however, in *The Century of*

_____

[6] Charles Darwin, *On the Origin of Species by Means of Natural Selection, or the Preservation of Favored Races in the Struggle for Life* (London: John Murray, 1859).

the Gene makes clear how human understanding of the nature and function of genes has significantly evolved over the years.[7] It is now generally recognized that genes vary considerably in the role that they play in different organisms depending upon how the organism in which they are located responds to varying environmental factors. For example, organisms in a given environment tend to co-create "ecological niches" in which to better survive and prosper.[8] But then the genes in each organism have to likewise adjust to an ever-changing physical environment so as to remain "dominant" rather than "recessive" in the organism's self-reproduction.

In 1995 Stuart Kauffman published *At Home in the Universe,* presenting computer models of the emergence of protocells from nonliving molecules, given a sufficient amount of diversity and ongoing dynamic interrelation.[9] It became clear to him that under the right conditions these inanimate molecules spontaneously co-produce "a self-sustaining network of reactions—an autocatalytic metabolism."[10] A living entity, a protocell, has thus come into existence in a world of otherwise inanimate entities. Kauffman, however, did not speculate about the deeper philosophical implications of his theory. For example, Aristotelian-Thomistic metaphysics takes for granted that the substantial form of an organism determines its material constituents to be a specific kind of physical entity.[11] But instead, according to Kauffman, the material components of a cell under certain circumstances produce the cell as a higher-order

---

[7] Evelyn Fox Keller, *The Century of the Gene* (Cambridge, MA: Harvard University Press, 2000), 66–72, 133–48.

[8] See Celia Deane-Drummond, *The Wisdom of the Liminal: Evolution and Other Animals in Human Becoming* (Grand Rapids, MI: Eerdmans, 2014), 219–22.

[9] Stuart Kauffman, *At Home in the Universe: The Search for the Laws of Self-Organization and Complexity* (New York: Oxford University Press, 1995), 3–30.

[10] Ibid., 47.

[11] Aristotle, *Metaphysics,* trans. Hippocrates G. Apostle (Grinnell, IA: Peripatetic Press, 1979), 1029a.

emergent reality that is alive rather than like themselves, inert mini-entities. Causation in the birth of a cell or mini-organism is then for the most part "bottom up" (in and through the interaction of the material constituents) rather than "top down" (in and through the higher-order activity of an immaterial substantial form as in classical metaphysics).

In 2012 Terrence Deacon of the University of California–Berkeley published *Incomplete Nature: How Mind Emerged from Matter.* In this book he consciously rejected the classical Aristotelian-Thomistic understanding of form and matter whereby causation is basically top down rather than bottom up. In Deacon's mind "being alive does not merely consist in being composed in a particular way. It consists in *changing* in a particular way"[12] He had in mind the ongoing interplay of thermodynamic, morphodynamic and teleodynamic systems within nature to explain the emergence of higher-order systems out of lower-order systems. To be specific, a thermodynamic system by itself tends to move toward complete equilibrium in line with the law of entropy.[13] But when two thermodynamic systems interact, they sometimes co-constitute a new morphodynamic system with a higher-order mode of operation that puts further constraints or limitations on the normal mode of operation of these two constituent thermodynamic subsystems.[14] For example, atoms by their ongoing interaction produce the higher-order reality of a molecule, but at a price. That is, they find their previous mode of operation as "free" atoms now constrained by the overarching mode of operation or governing structure of the molecule. Finally, when two or more morphodynamic systems interact, they sometimes produce a new teleodynamic system with an inbuilt directionality or goal orientation that over time is responsible for the emergence of

---

[12] Terrence W. Deacon, *Incomplete Nature: How Mind Emerged from Matter* (New York: W. W. Norton, 2012), 175.

[13] Ibid., 227–34.

[14] Ibid., 261.

sensate life in animal species and self-consciousness or rational life in human beings.[15]

Deacon's account of higher-order systems as emergent out of the interplay of lower-order systems within physical reality is remarkably close to Whitehead's analysis in *Process and Reality* of the interplay between the governing structure of a society and the constituent actual entities of the society to produce over time a more complex structured society, that is, a society composed of interrelated sub-societies.[16] But Deacon and Whitehead differ on one major point. For Whitehead, the ultimate constituents of a society (actual entities) are living; for Deacon, the ultimate constituents of systems (atoms and molecules) are nonliving. For Deacon, as a result, there is the paradox of nonlife producing life: "Real teleological and intentional phenomena can emerge from physical and chemical processes previously devoid of these properties."[17] For Whitehead, there is no paradox because all actual entities are alive, subjects of experience, not inanimate mini-things. Here I align myself with Whitehead in claiming that higher levels of life come from lower levels of life. Admittedly, within higher-order societies or systems the constituent actual entities are more complex and self-aware than the actual entities in lower-order societies or systems.[18] But the components of every society and system without exception are alive, subjects of experience responsive to one another and to the external environment.

Jesper Hoffmeyer, a leading figure in the relatively new field of biosemiotics, is more willing than Deacon to allow for signs of life among the constituents of biochemical systems. For, as he sees it, between these entities information is traded by way

---

[15] Ibid., 319–25.

[16] Whitehead, *Process and Reality*, 90–91, 99. See also Chapter 2 herein.

[17] Deacon, *Incomplete Nature*, 323.

[18] Whitehead, *Process and Reality*, 177–78.

of signs that have to be interpreted in order to be understood.[19] Furthermore, this trading of information seems to exist even at the level of molecules as the constituents of cells.[20] Hoffmeyer is reluctant, however, to go further and endorse Whitehead's notion of actual entities as momentary self-constituting subjects of experience that exchange signs ("prehensions" in Whitehead's terminology) with one another from moment to moment.[21] This reluctance on Hoffmeyer's part is somewhat curious since his intellectual mentor in the field of biosemiotics is Charles Sanders Peirce, whose philosophy is based on the analysis and interpretation of different kinds of signs. For Peirce was also convinced that mind and matter are closely interwoven, virtually interchangeable: "Matter is effete mind, inveterate habits becoming physical laws."[22] So Peirce presupposes what Hoffmeyer denies, namely, that habit forming and therefore some form of protomental activity is characteristic of entities at all levels of existence and activity within physical reality.[23]

Critique of Scientific Explanations of Systems

In retrospect, then, Kauffman, Deacon, and Hoffmeyer have effectively challenged one of the main presuppositions of early modern natural science, that is, that physical entities can be reduced to the ongoing interaction of their ultimate constituents,

---

[19] Jesper Hoffmeyer, *Biosemiotics: An Examination into the Signs of Life and the Life of Signs,* trans. Jesper Hoffmeyer and Donald Favareau, ed. Donald Favareau (Scranton, PA: Scranton University Press, 2008), 3–5.

[20] Ibid., 31–37, 195–97.

[21] Personal communication, email.

[22] Charles Hartshorne and Paul Weiss, eds., *Collected Papers of Charles Sanders Peirce,* vol. 6 (Cambridge, MA: Harvard University Press, 1935), 25.

[23] Likewise, Deacon appeals to Peirce's notion of habit-taking in his explanation of the origin and growth of systems in *Incomplete Nature,* 183–85.

namely, atoms understood as inert bits of matter pushed and pulled in different directions by external forces (for example, gravity and electromagnetism). Kauffman, Deacon, and Hoffmeyer have instead claimed that genuinely new higher-order systems are emergent out of the ongoing interplay of lower-order systems in a way that is not reducible to the ongoing interaction of their ultimate constituent parts or members. What emerges are systems with new properties and a mode of operation different from the mode of operation of the constituent sub-systems in isolation from one another.

But Kauffman, Deacon, and Hoffmeyer have not then concluded that the atomic and molecular components of cells are likewise alive, capable of spontaneous interaction with one another so as to bring about the emergence of the genuinely new higher-order physical reality of the cell. Deacon, for example, is clearly worried about being accused of panpsychism, that is, belief in "mind all the way down."[24] Material reality is instead a mirage or an illusion. The ancient belief that there is a mental component even in a grain of sand is in their minds definitively disproven by modern natural science. But, as the well-known scholar in the field of world religions Huston Smith commented years ago, while what is empirically measurable is unquestionably true, to further claim that only what is empirically measurable is true is to be guilty of scientism, a loss of the full richness of physical reality.[25] Philosopher of science Thomas Nagel would agree: "Mind and everything that goes with it is inherent in the universe."[26] Nagel is not a student of Whitehead's philosophy largely because in his mind Whitehead as a philosophical atomist was breaking up the unity of mind into its "protomental parts."[27] Yet Nagel still agrees with

---

[24] Ibid., 72–73.

[25] Huston Smith, *Forgotten Truth: The Primordial Tradition* (New York: Harper and Row, 1976), 14–18.

[26] Thomas Nagel, *Mind and Cosmos: Why the Materialist Neo-Darwinian Conception of Nature Is Almost Certainly False* (New York: Oxford University Press, 2012), 15.

[27] Ibid., 87–88.

Whitehead that "physics and chemistry cannot fully account for life and consciousness."[28]

The Understanding of the Christian God-World Relationship in Today's World

Many Christian philosophers and theologians rely on the classical Aristotelian-Thomistic understanding of the God-world relationship even though both Aristotle and Thomas Aquinas were understandably completely unaware of the evolutionary character of physical reality. Both lived in what seemed to be a relatively stable world with a prefixed hierarchy of beings (individual entities). Aquinas, for example, claimed that God is the Supreme Being. Thus God transcends the world of creation even though God is also active in the world as its Creator and Sustainer. God is then the First Cause of everything else that exists through God's knowledge and love of all finite entities and through God's power to make things happen in the world of creation.[29] Furthermore, as a strictly immaterial reality, God does not take up space and thereby exclude other entities from occupying the same spatial location.[30] Yet there are unresolved philosophical issues with this understanding of the God-world relationship. For example, God's knowledge and love of creatures is part of God's own subjective experience of creation and thus may or may not be directly experienced by creatures as well. God's power vis-à-vis creation is necessarily felt by creatures because they come into being and continue to exist only by the power of God. But the doctrine of creation is still a religious belief, not an established scientific fact. For, the world may also exist in virtue of its own power of being, for example, creativity in Whitehead's scheme.

---

[28] Ibid., 8.

[29] Aquinas, *Summa theologiae*, I, Q. 8, art. 3, resp.

[30] Ibid., I, Q. 8, art. 2 resp.

Furthermore, even if creatures exist in and through the power of God, are they as a result powerless to do anything other than what God wants? Thomas Aquinas and other classical metaphysicians distinguished between the primary causality of God and the secondary causality of creatures, above all human beings and other higher-order animal species.[31] God makes some things happen directly but brings about the existence and activity of lower-order things through causal powers innate in higher-order creatures.[32] Thus human beings are consciously or more often unconsciously the instruments of God in bringing about the divine plan for creation.[33] Yet, if human beings and other creatures are the instruments of divine Providence, is God then responsible for the existence of both natural and moral evil in this world? Whitehead resolved this problem by claiming that God is only the principle of limitation within the cosmic process.[34] But for Whitehead, God is then only a component in the cosmic process, not its Creator and Sustainer as in classical metaphysics. So Whitehead's metaphysics evades one philosophical problem by creating another. Is any other explanation of the God-world relationship available?

Panentheism

Given conceptual problems with the classical God-world relationship, some contemporary Christian philosophers and theologians have begun thinking of God's relation to the world in terms of panentheism, the belief that everything exists in God but at the same time is distinct from God in its own finite mode of existence and activity. But, as the Danish theologian and philosopher of science Niels Henrik Gregersen comments,

---

[31] Ibid., I, Q. 22, art. 3, ad 2.

[32] Ibid., I, Q. 22, art. 4 resp.

[33] Ibid., I, Q. 22, art. 3, ad 1.

[34] Alfred North Whitehead, *Science and the Modern World* (New York: Free Press, 1967), 178–79.

"The concept of panentheism is not stable in itself."[35] Everything depends upon what one means by the word *in*. Gregersen favors the idea that "there exists a real two-way interaction between God and the world, so that (1) the world is somehow 'contained in God' and (2) there will be some 'return' of the world into the life of God."[36] Panentheism, accordingly, is distinct both from monism (no difference between God and the world) and classical theism (major difference between God and the world). An example of panentheism that tends toward monism is the claim that God is the soul of the world and the world is the body of God. That is, God permeates the world like the soul or life-principle of the body, but the world as the body of God is necessary for God to be God. God is never without the coexistence of a world (not necessarily this world, but some world) in order to be God: "God is the compound individual who at all times has embraced or will embrace the fullness of all other individuals existing at those times. He is the only eternal individual."[37] Sallie McFague likes the model of God as the soul of the world since it makes clear that God shares the pain of creatures. But she still finds it awkward to think of oneself as, in effect, a body part of God.[38] She instead favors an interpersonal model of God as alternately Mother, Lover, and Friend. Yet these terms do not designate for McFague distinct Persons (technically, subsistent relations) within one God as in the Christian doctrine of the Trinity but are simply three different finite models or analogies for the activity of God in human life.[39]

---

[35] Niels Henrik Gregersen, "Three Varieties of Panentheism," in *In Whom We Live and Move and Have Our Being: Panentheistic Reflections in a Scientific World*, ed. Philip Clayton and Arthur Peacocke (Grand Rapids, MI: Eerdmans, 2004), 19.

[36] Ibid., 20.

[37] Charles Hartshorne, "The Compound Individual," *Philosophical Essays for Alfred North Whitehead* (New York: Russell and Russell, 1936), 218.

[38] Sallie McFague, *Models of God: Theology for an Ecological, Nuclear Age* (Philadelphia: Fortress Press, 1987), 75.

[39] Ibid., 78–87.

Neo-Thomists and other classically oriented theists, however, in my judgment, end up with something close to a dualistic understanding of the God-world relationship. For, in trying to explain what they mean by panentheism in terms of a modern, process-oriented approach to the God-world relationship, they still largely adhere to principles of classical metaphysics. The results are quite uneven. For concepts that are perfectly intelligible within one systematic understanding of the God-world relationship tend to be ambiguous if not incoherent within a rival thought system. Certainly, the full intelligibility of the God-world relationship is beyond human comprehension, but some explanations of that relationship make more sense than others. Simply to make my point here, I offer some brief comments on the work of two colleagues and friends who lean toward a more dynamic, process-oriented understanding of the God-world relationship but still explain it in the language and concepts of classical metaphysics.

Two Neo-Thomistic Approaches

Australian theologian Denis Edwards claims, in line with an evolutionary understanding of physical reality, that God should be seen "not simply as the dynamic cause of the *existence* of creatures [as in classical metaphysics], but as the dynamic ground of their *becoming*."[40] But then one must ask how God can be both transcendent of the cosmic process as in classical metaphysics and at the same time the immanent ground or organizing principle of activity for creatures in an evolutionary context. As I see it, the only way to resolve that speculative problem is to distinguish between the personhood of God as a strictly transcendent reality and the nature of God as the self-organizing principle of activity within the divine Life and by extension likewise within the cosmic process. But is that possible within the parameters of Thomas Aquinas's

---

[40] Denis Edwards, "A Relational and Evolving Universe Unfolding within the Dynamism of the Divine Communion," in Clayton and Peacocke, *In Whom We Live and Move and Have Our Being*, 208.

understanding of the Trinity in the *Summa theologiae?* For Aquinas claimed therein that each of the divine Persons is the full reality of God, albeit from one relational perspective: as Father, or as Son, or as Holy Spirit.[41] This appears to be, if not a logical contradiction, then at least a notable exception to the traditional understanding of the proper relation between the rival concepts of nature and person in human experience. All human beings share one and the same human nature, but they are at the same time separate individuals. As a result, Edwards ends up being more dualistic in his thinking than he apparently realizes. For in God there is no difference between the nature of God and the reality of God as an individual entity. But in the world of creation individual entities of the same type or species routinely share one and the same nature or essence as their common principle of existence and activity. Hence, there is no realistic analogy between who and what God is vis-à-vis who and what human beings are. God and human beings are totally different kinds of entities who as a result necessarily live in separate worlds of existence and activity.

Similarly, in *Breath of Life*, Edwards appeals to the theology of Basil, one of the three Cappadocian fathers of the church, to explain how God, specifically the Holy Spirit, is the "place" in which the saints "dwell."[42] In this way the Holy Spirit "is the Communion-Bringer and, as such, is the Life-Giver and Sanctifier."[43] Yet in the world of creation a "place" is only the context or setting for the interaction of entities; it is not itself one of the entities in interaction. German theologian Wolfhart Pannenberg, in the first volume of *Systematic Theology*, makes this necessary distinction between place and entities in a given place as part of his analysis of the ontological difference between the nature of God as the divine Spirit as opposed to the

---

[41] Aquinas, *Summa theologiae* I, Q. 29, art. 4, resp.
[42] Denis Edwards, *Breath of Life: A Theology of the Creator Spirit* (Maryknoll, NY: Orbis Books, 2004), 29.
[43] Ibid.

Holy Spirit as one of the three divine Persons existing in the Spirit.[44]

Elizabeth Johnson seems to be guilty of some of the same logical ambiguity in her use of key terms in her book *She Who Is*. Therein she claims that all three divine Persons are self-expressions or manifestations of Sophia (divine Wisdom) as "the creative, relational power of being who enlivens, suffers with, sustains, and enfolds the universe."[45] Yet is Sophia in this citation a noun or a verb, that is, an entity or an activity? If it is an entity, then it is presumably another name for the Holy Spirit. But the Holy Spirit is a divine Person and thus by nature transcendent of the world of creation, not immanent within it as its principle of potentiality or change. If, however, Sophia as "the creative, relational power of being" is an activity and not an entity, then it should logically be the principle of activity within the divine Life as well as within the world of creation, thereby linking the divine Persons to one another as co-constituents of a transcendent community. But, as already noted, in Aquinas's explanation of the Trinity in the *Summa theologiae*, the nature of God is identical with the reality of God as a transcendent individual entity. For Aquinas, then, the divine nature is not a principle of activity—as nature or essence is in the self-constitution of finite entities—but simply another name for the reality of God as *Ipsum Esse Subsistens*, the pure act of existence without further qualification.

Here too, of course, I am not criticizing Johnson any more than Edwards for trying to rethink the Christian God-world relationship in process-oriented and relational terms. I applaud them both for that move but feel obliged to remind them that they have then consciously or unconsciously moved from the classical metaphysics of being based on unilateral cause-effect relations between individual entities to a contemporary

---

[44] Wolfhart Pannenberg, *Systematic Theology,* vol. 1, trans. Geoffrey W. Bromiley (Grand Rapids, MI: Eerdmans, 1991), 427–32.

[45] Elizabeth A. Johnson, *She Who Is: The Mystery of God in Feminist Theological Discourse* (New York: Crossroad Press, 1992), 13.

metaphysics of becoming based on the ongoing dynamic interrelation of processes or systems of entities to one another. Moving successfully from one metaphysical system to another is, in other words, very tricky. One has to avoid the temptation to oversimplify that transition process through use of images or metaphors that are in themselves easy to understand but do not offer anything like a systematic explanation or rational argument for reconciliation of two significantly different worldviews.

A Systems-Oriented Approach to Panentheism

At this point in the chapter I set forth my own panentheistic understanding of the God-world relationship in which finite entities come forth from God, continue to exist by the power of God during their time on this earth, and eventually are reincorporated into the divine Life so as to continue to exist in a transformed state after death. I make four basic metaphysical assumptions here. First of all, I agree with Deacon that systems can be merged with other systems so as to bring about in some cases the emergence of new higher-order systems in a way that still allows for the continuing existence of the lower-order systems in their own specific mode of operation. Second, I agree with Whitehead that the ultimate components of these systems are not inanimate entities but self-determining subjects of experience (actual entities) so that the system as a whole is not completely deterministic but in varying degrees open-ended in its mode of operation. Third, I agree with Deacon once again that, while both top-down and bottom-up causation are involved in the ongoing mode of operation of systems, bottom-up causation is more important because it allows for the gradual evolution of lower-order systems into higher-order systems within physical reality. Finally, I argue that within a Christian understanding of the God-world, the topmost system is the starting point, not the end point, of the evolutionary cosmic process.

I begin with that last assumption, namely, that in the Christian God-world relationship the topmost system does not come into existence at the end of the cosmic process but is located at the beginning of that process as its necessary starting point. Thus God as Trinity is the starting point of the cosmic process. That is, the triune God is a corporate life-system composed of three dynamically interrelated individual life-systems, the systematic unity-in-diversity of Father, Son, and Holy Spirit. This understanding of the Trinity basically corresponds to what Whitehead calls a structured society, a society composed of sub-societies.[46] Physical reality is likewise full of such structured societies. For example, all the different organs at work in the human body are sub-societies or sub-systems within the human body, and yet each retains its own distinctive mode of operation as heart, lungs, brain, and so on. Similarly, a human community is a higher-order, corporately organized system in its own right even as it is sustained in existence by human beings as individual lower-order systems in dynamic interrelation.

But if God is a corporate or socially organized reality, then the world of creation as the finite expression of the *imago Dei* should likewise be a socially organized reality, namely, a higher-order system composed of multiple ongoing lower-order systems. So, whereas in classical metaphysics the individual human being was the *imago Dei*, within this process-oriented understanding of the God-world relationship, it is corporate realities or systems that are the image of God as a corporate life-system or divine community. This is, of course, not to deny the key role of individual entities in the workings of a given process or system. For, as noted above, the ultimate constituents of a given system are self-constituting subjects of experience in dynamic interrelation. Accordingly, the system is not deterministic in its mode of operation but open-ended, capable of evolutionary change both internally and externally—internally in virtue of the ever-changing relation of constituent actual entities to one another within the system; externally in

---

[46] Whitehead, *Process and Reality*, 99.

terms of the ever-changing relation of those same constituent actual entities to their counterparts in other nearby systems.[47]

My systems-oriented approach to the God-world relationship thus begins with the presupposition that the topmost system is the divine Life-system constituted by the ongoing dynamic interrelation of the divine Persons with one another. I then argue that the world of creation was historically emergent out of the all-encompassing field of activity proper to the divine Persons in their interaction with one another from moment to moment. This energy field proper to the divine Persons, accordingly, was and still is the vital source or primordial energy field for the gradual emergence of the world of creation as a hierarchically ordered set of systems, each with its own ontological integrity and mode of operation. Theoretical physicists refer to this starting point of the cosmic process as the Big Bang. I only add that the Big Bang took place within the "space" of the structured field of activity proper to the divine Persons. But, as a result, the structure and ongoing mode of operation of the divine Life-system sets boundaries or constraints on the way that the cosmic process took shape and over time continues to evolve. At the same time, the inner workings of the cosmic process are not thereby fully determined by divine Providence. Since the ultimate constituents of all the finite systems within creation are subjects of experience that make their own self-constituting "decisions" from moment to moment on how to function within the parameters set by the all-inclusive divine Life-system, there is still considerable spontaneity and unpredictability in how the cosmic process de facto will proceed from moment to moment.

There is, in other words, a reciprocal causality at work in the relation of the divine Persons with their creatures and in the

---

[47] The degree of open-endedness of the society or system in its mode of operation varies, of course, depending on its size and complexity. The open-endedness in the mode of operation of an atom or molecule is trivial by comparison with the open-endedness in the thinking and behavior of an adult human being with full self-awareness from moment to moment.

relation of the creatures of this world with the divine Persons. The distinction between the primary causality of God and the secondary causality of creatures no longer really holds since the divine Persons and their creatures are mutually responsive to one another's initiative in a way that is inconsistent with the ontological priority of divine primary causality over creaturely secondary causality in classical metaphysics. Likewise, there is no sharp distinction between the natural order and the supernatural order of events within cosmic history, since responsibility for what happens is shared in different ways by the divine Persons with their creatures. For example, during his earthly life Jesus functioned as a divine Person with both a divine and human nature. Yet the divine nature and the human nature of Jesus worked together to produce one and the same empirical effect in the life of Jesus from moment to moment. For, in some of his words and actions, Jesus clearly exhibited divine power (for example, curing a blind man or healing a woman of internal hemorrhaging). But in other ways Jesus in his words and actions exhibited the limitations of life in the body (physically, hunger and fatigue; psychologically, joy and sadness, enthusiasm and discouragement). But, if this is how the divine and the human consistently worked together in the life of Jesus, is it not likely that nature and grace subtly work together to produce one and the same effect in the thoughts, words, and actions of all other human beings as well?

Recently Danish philosopher of science and theologian Niels Henrik Gregersen proposed the notion of "deep incarnation": God taking flesh not only in the humanity of Jesus but also in the cosmic process as a whole.[48] I fully agree with him on this point but further argue that the Incarnation of God into the cosmic process then began with the Big Bang, the primordial explosion of divine Energy out of the structured field of activity proper to the divine Persons in their ongoing dynamic inter-relationship. Likewise, the incarnation of Jesus is best seen,

---

[48] Niels Henrik Gregersen, "*Cur deus caro?* Jesus and the Cosmos Story," *Theology and Science* 11, no. 4 (2013): 370–93.

not as a singular event in human history, but as the divinely intended high point or climax of the historical incorporation of the cosmic process into the divine Life-system that will be fully accomplished only at the end of the world when all of creation will be linked with the divine Persons within the kingdom of God in its final state. But is this wishful thinking on my part? At the beginning of his letter to the Ephesians and then in his letter to the Colossians, Saint Paul claims that this is indeed God's plan for the fullness of times, "to sum up all things in Christ, in heaven and on earth" (Eph 1:10). But can this religious belief also be rationally justified? In what follows, I suggest that a systems-oriented approach to reality is far more plausible than other alternatives to justify this claim made by Paul in Ephesians and Colossians.

Life after Death

I begin with a reminder from Whitehead that processes or systems are constituted by actual entities as momentary self-constituting subjects of experience with "a common element of form" or governing structure that itself gradually changes in response to the dynamic interplay of its constituent actual entities from moment to moment.[49] Hence, that which endures over time is not a physical entity in the Aristotelian sense but only the evolving dominant pattern in the mode of operation of a process or system (understood as a series of dynamically interrelated events). That is, whereas in classical metaphysics individual entities survive the passage of time essentially unchanged with only accidental changes in response to various external circumstances, in a systems-oriented or process-oriented worldview only the dominant pattern in the succession of events within a society or system survives the passage of time. By implication, then, what is carried forward in a human being's transit from life in this world to eternal life within the divine Life-system is the enduring pattern of one's earthly life,

---

[49] Whitehead, *Process and Reality*, 90–91.

namely, those habits of thinking, speaking, and acting that have gradually defined one's personality or ontological identity in this life. The physical body dies, but its prevailing pattern of existence and activity over the years of its mortal life is incorporated into the historical pattern of the all-encompassing divine Life-system.

English philosopher and theologian John Polkinghorne makes approximately the same point about what survives from moment to moment in a person's life:

> We have very few atoms in our bodies today that were there even two years ago. What does appear to be the carrier of continuity is the immensely complex "information-bearing pattern" in which that matter is organized. The pattern is not static; it is modified as we acquire new experiences, insights and memories, in accordance with the dynamic of our living history. It is this information-bearing pattern that is the soul.[50]

If then, as Polkinghorne claims, the soul of a human being is not an immaterial entity joined to a material body at the moment of conception but instead the "information-bearing pattern" within the body-soul totality of a human being, what happens at the moment of death? In terms of my own systems-oriented approach to the God-world relationship, two dynamically interrelated events simultaneously take place at the moment of death so as to allow a human being to enjoy both objective and subjective immortality within the divine Life. First, at the moment of death one will realize for the first time that what one said and did over the years has been progressively incorporated into the ongoing history of the kingdom of

---

[50] John Polkinghorne, *The God of Hope and the End of the World* (New Haven, CT: Yale University Press, 2002), 106. Polkinghorne is a conscientious Christian as well as a natural scientist. Thus he believes in Christ's resurrection from the dead, the bodily resurrection of all human beings, and the transformation of the cosmic process into a "new creation" (2 Cor 5:17) at the end of the world.

God, that is, the Life-system proper to the three divine Persons that has always existed and will never cease to exist. Second, since at the moment of death one is free from the limiting conditions of life in a physical body, one will comprehend in a flash of insight the overall role that one de facto played in salvation history. This, of course, will be a moment of personal judgment in that one will see for the first time how much or how little one actually contributed to the fulfillment of the enduring goals and values of the kingdom of God during one's earthly life. Thus one will be faced with a fateful decision: either to embrace one's past life with overflowing thanks to the divine Persons for their acceptance of oneself as a repentant sinner, or to reject the meaning and value of one's life as recorded within salvation history and choose instead to live apart from the divine Persons and all those human beings who have accepted the full truth of their lives on earth. As Polkinghorne further comments in his own discussion of the four last things, "Hell is a place of boredom rather than a place of unending torture" (as in the descriptions of hell in the scriptures).[51]

Heaven, however, will not be an unchanging state of bliss as a result of having achieved one's goal in life, but rather the beginning of a new set of enriching interpersonal experiences with the three divine Persons and one's fellow creatures within the fullness of the kingdom of God, the everlasting divine Life-system.[52] As for life after death for nonhuman creatures, they too will presumably possess objective immortality within the everlasting kingdom of God or divine Life-system because they also contributed to the ongoing history of the kingdom of God. But nonhuman creatures will likely possess subjective immortality only on a feeling level, that is, in terms of an innate feeling of well-being and/or satisfaction in being part of a reality greater than themselves as individual entities. Likewise, presumably not all nonhuman creatures will enjoy a subjective sense of well-being to the same degree. A long-lived animal, for

---

[51] Ibid., 136–37.
[52] Ibid., 132–33.

example, may have a sufficiently strong sense of self-identity so as to enjoy life after death more fully than an insect whose lifespan and limited subjective activity can be measured in terms of days or at most weeks, not years.

The point of these reflections on what is likely in store for human beings and the other creatures of this world at the end of their earthly lives is, however, not to claim any privileged knowledge of the future. Instead I only propose that this approach to Christian belief in life after death is rationally plausible, that is, generally consistent with a philosophical interpretation of physical reality that contemporary natural scientists like Stuart Kauffman, Terrence Deacon, and Jesper Hoffmeyer embrace as the way the cosmic process works. Rational plausibility, of course, is never proof of a theory, but it is certainly better than the presentation of one's religious beliefs in an idiom that contemporary natural and social scientists would find very difficult to understand and accept.

In the next chapter I extend these reflections on a systems-oriented understanding of reality to indicate in more detail how the three divine Persons influenced but did not directly control the birth and historical development of the early church as both a new religiously oriented life-system and as an institutional entity with a strong hierarchically organized structure of authority. I will also indicate how the Roman Catholic Church currently seems to be undergoing an identity crisis in that, as a result of differing declarations about the nature of the church at Vatican II, conservatives and liberals seem to be pulling in different directions vis-à-vis the future of the church. Accordingly, in line with my systems-oriented approach to church life and organization, I set forth a compromise position on the nature of the church by focusing on the changing role of ministry in the life of the church. Properly understood, ministry in and for the church can be the responsibility of all Christians and yet be exercised in different ways, depending upon the role that the individual Christian plays in the organizational structure of the local church.

Chapter 4

Church: Both Life-System and Institutional Entity

As I noted in the Introduction, the first three chapters of this book are dedicated to the construction of a new, systems-oriented worldview or cosmology that is conducive to setting forth in Chapter 4 and Chapter 5 a new understanding of the church as a historical process, that is, a corporate life-system, as well as a stable institutional entity with a fixed structure of authority and mode of operation. My basic argument for this line of thought is that, if the world is constituted by different kinds of life-systems in dynamic relation to one another, it makes good sense to see the church as likewise a life-system, one among the innumerable other life-systems that together make up the cosmic process as an all-comprehensive corporate life-system. Furthermore, as mentioned in Chapter 3, the cosmic process itself is a sub-system or finite constituent of the even more comprehensive divine Life-system. Hence, the three divine Persons of the Christian doctrine of the Trinity acting conjointly as a corporate life-system directly influence but do not fully control everything that happens in the cosmic process as well as in the ongoing life of the church. Divine Providence for the world of creation is, accordingly, just as real as in the traditional Christian God-world relationship. But the divine Persons in this systems-oriented God-world relationship act on creation much more indirectly through a new kind of formal causality within the cosmic process, namely, the inevitable constraints exercised by the empirically grounded laws of nature and the ever-changing historical structures of life in close contact with others. Likewise, they employ a new kind of final causality based on persuasion rather than divine primary efficient causality in dealing with their creatures as in classical metaphysics.

In a word, what I am suggesting with this scheme is that the three divine Persons deal with us on a regular basis much more through the systems in which we live, move, and have our being than with us simply as isolated individuals. For example, part of our traditional Christian heritage is the belief that we are members of the mystical body of Christ. But how does that cohere with another traditional Christian belief that we are in the first place individual persons endowed with inalienable rights vis-à-vis other human beings? As I point out below, to participate fully in the corporate reality of the church and of the mystical body of Christ one has to be a free person with responsibilities both to self and others. So finding one's personal identity through active participation in the system(s) to which one belongs is not in any sense a logical contradiction but instead the affirmation of a higher-order truth, the truth of one's place in a greater, socially constituted reality. If the divine Persons themselves exist as individuals only insofar as they together co-constitute the divine Life-system, why should we human beings be any different?

Here one might well object that this shift in focus from the individual as an entity existing in its own right to the more complicated notion of the individual as necessarily existing in community with other individuals may be risky. After all, the concept of the individual as an entity existing in its own right, and at the human level a person with inalienable human rights vis-à-vis others, is one of the great achievements of Western civilization and should not be lost sight of for the sake of something new and untested. My counterargument is twofold. First of all, as the Protestant theologian Walter Rauschenbusch claimed in *A Theology for the Social Gospel* years ago, the traditional focus of Christianity in Western civilization has been on the need for the individual to be redeemed from a life of sin in and through the passion, death, and resurrection of Jesus as the incarnate Word of God. Yet, says Rauschenbusch, Jesus himself in the gospel narrative stressed reform of the structures of society in the Judaism of his day and was eventually arrested and put to death for that same reason.[1] Within the Roman Catholic community, Gustavo Gutiérrez in *A Theology of Liberation* emphasized the pertinence of Jesus's gospel message for the poor people of Latin America in their ongoing struggle to be free of oppressive economic, political, and social structures that had been imposed upon them by the upper classes of Latin American society.[2] Both of these books were quite influential in their own day. Gutiérrez's book was certainly a reference point in the composition of the decrees of Vatican II, notably *Gaudium et spes (Pastoral Constitution on the Church in the Modern World)*. Yet it seems safe to say that average contemporary Christians still think largely in terms of their personal salvation as the goal of the Christian life. So a fresh focus on the responsibility of individual Christians for the prosperity and continued well-being of the political, economic, and social order of their day should be welcomed rather than regarded with suspicion by Christians in all walks of life.

Second, as Anglican theologian Colin Gunton noted in *The One, the Three, and the Many*, the culture of modernity is shot through with an exaggerated focus on the individual human being as the center of his or her own private world of experience.[3] Yet the more one tries to assert oneself as a particular individual, the more one loses one's real difference from others.

---

[1] Walter Rauschenbusch, *A Theology for the Social Gospel* (New York: Abingdon Press, 1917), 1–9, 95–109, 118–30.

[2] Gustavo Gutiérrez, *A Theology of Liberation: History, Politics and Salvation*, trans. Sister Coridad Inda and John Eagleson (Maryknoll, NY: Orbis Books, 1988), 97–105, 174.

[3] Colin E. Gunton, *The One, the Three, and the Many: God, Creation, and the Culture of Modernity* (Cambridge, UK: Cambridge University Press, 1993), 1–73.

Ironically, everyone tries to be different in much the same way. True individuality is to be found in identifying oneself with and contributing to a socially constituted reality greater than oneself. That socially constituted reality should not be some finite cause or social movement that is worthwhile but not deserving of one's complete dedication and/or worship. In Gunton's trinitarian cosmology, "Spirit enables a form of perichoresis to take place, between mind and world, world and God."[4] I made a similar argument in Chapter 3 when I set forth my systems-oriented approach to the God-world relationship, in which human beings are participants in successively higher-order systems within the cosmic process and ultimately incorporated into the divine Life-system. So, not only to deal with the current problem of exaggerated individualism in Western culture but also to anchor contemporary life in the church within a more explicitly trinitarian context than in the past, I feel justified in setting forth my argument in this chapter.

Hence, in the first part of the chapter I offer a brief overview of the history of the church from its beginnings in the apostolic era of the church up to and including Vatican I. My intent here is to make clear that the popes and bishops had to work hard to assert the necessary independence of the church from the ambitions of at least some of the secular rulers of Western society in the Middle Ages and thus inadvertently ended up with an overemphasis on the church as an institutional entity rather than as a faith community or religiously oriented life-system. In the second part of the chapter I offer my evaluation of a movement both at Vatican II and in the years that followed in the direction of a new understanding of the church as a dynamic life-system as well as a strong institutional entity. Finally, in the third part of the chapter I focus on one key way to keep alive this new understanding of the church as a dynamic life-system in which all Christians can be actively involved. What I have in mind is a fresh focus on a relational approach to a theology of ministry in which ministries are exercised in the local parish by

---

[4] Ibid., 185.

lay staff and lay volunteers as well as by the pastor and other ordained clergy (for example, deacons).

Church History from the Apostolic Era to Vatican I

Whether Jesus during his lifetime on earth explicitly wanted to found a new ecclesial body that would rival the Judaism of his day with the apostle Peter as its initial head is a matter of scholarly debate. It is not clear that the reference to church in Matthew's Gospel (Matt 16:18) pertains to the specific community of Jewish Christians to which Matthew's Gospel was primarily addressed to assist them in their relations with orthodox Jews in the same civil community or to the church everywhere in the Mediterranean world at that time. In either case in the rest of Matthew's Gospel and in the other gospel narratives, Jesus seems to be more focused on a much-needed reform of the Judaism of his day along the lines of more freedom of thought and a more spontaneous lifestyle on the part of his followers and their friends and neighbors. Hence, Jesus may be better seen as the guiding force in a new religious movement within Judaism rather than as the founder of a new religious body.[5] In any case, as church historian Bernard Prusak points out, "The early communities were tentative, provisional, and free to experiment in regard to their own order and structure, and in relation to the particularities of various moments and contexts."[6]

At the same time, the gospel message had to be preached to a largely Gentile population that was already being offered "salvation" in terms of other religious movements of the day, e.g., Gnosticism with its focus on the life of the mind and

---

[5] Richard R. Gaillardetz, *Ecclesiology for a Global Church: A People Called and Sent* (Maryknoll, NY: Orbis Books, 2008), 17–18.

[6] Bernard Prusak, *The Church Unfinished: Ecclesiology through the Centuries* (New York: Paulist Press, 2004), 56. In the following I give the page number of the text of *The Church Unfinished* in parentheses wherever needed.

corresponding contempt for the body.[7] Hence, it was altogether natural for the early Christian communities to look to the guidance of their bishop as successor to one of the apostles for discerning the difference between their faith and the teachings of these other religious sects. As a result an informal theology of tradition quickly developed with focus on the authority of an *episcopos* or other ordained church member in the community. Yet in those early centuries of the church's existence, tradition was not seen in a formal sense as a complement or a rival to scripture as in the years after the Council of Trent in the sixteenth century. Tradition included "the whole living Gospel in all of its various historical embodiments" (for example, the example of martyrs, the witness of ordinary believers, the celebration of the liturgy and the sacraments, theological reflection and Christian art).[8] In brief, then, in the first two centuries of the church's existence there was relatively little formal structure and, as noted above, considerable freedom in adjusting to different contexts. At the same time, there was a strong sense of solidarity among the early Christian communities in the Mediterranean world. As Prusak notes in *The Church Unfinished*, "The catholic or universal Church was made present in every place through each church united in communion (or *koinonia*) with every other church" (120).

Growing Centralization of Church Authority

Appeals by local churches and local church councils to the authority of the bishop of Rome as the successor to the apostle Peter so as to settle disputed matters of doctrine, morals, and ritual propriety were, of course, periodically made. These appeals were made in the beginning on a somewhat informal basis, but with the passage of time on a more formal basis and as something to be expected. Pope Leo the Great (440–61), for example, "declared that whole world came to Peter's See, and

---

[7] Gaillardetz, *Ecclesiology for a Global Church*, 211.
[8] Ibid.

that the care of its bishop extended over the universal Church" (142). His views echoed comments made earlier by distinguished theologians like Augustine and Jerome. Cyprian of Carthage likewise endorsed the overall primacy of the church at Rome and the authority of its bishop over other bishops but, as Prusak comments, never endorsed the centralization of the church's authority around the person of the pope (136). Yet in retrospect, centralization of church authority and structure was inevitable once Christianity became the official religion of the Roman Empire. Many more people became converts to Christianity, with the result that many bishops became responsible for a network of local churches or parishes in which priests other than the bishop himself presided (155). Hence, slowly but surely the hierarchical structure of those ordained to church ministry (holy orders) was set in place: deacons, priests, bishops, archbishops, pope. Actual pastoral ministry to the laity was administrated by priests; bishops and archbishops became administrators of dioceses.

In the High Middle Ages this centralization of authority in the church became even more pronounced as local bishops found themselves in conflict with the civil ruler (a duke or other nobleman) in their diocese, not so much over matters of faith and morals but rather in terms of property ownership and jurisdiction over the commoners living on those properties. For, over the centuries, property rights were often deeded to bishops and pastors by wealthy Christians on their deathbed as a form of personal preparation for death and judgment. On the papal level it was instead the pope's dealings with the Holy Roman emperor that were at stake. The pope had the power to excommunicate the emperor and thereby to release the emperor's noblemen and commoners from obedience to his dictates. So the emperor had no choice but to seek reconciliation with the church in the person of the pope when his own right to rule over his subjects was threatened. This unusually close relation between the emperor and the pope actually began on Christmas Day, 800, when Pope Leo III crowned Charlemagne, formerly king of the Franks and Lombards, as the first emperor of Western Christendom, thereby uniting "all Western Christians in one Church and state, under one pope and one Christian emperor, crowned by the pope who was 'head' of the Church" (184). This sometimes testy relationship between pope and emperor reached its pinnacle with the decree *Unam sanctam* of Pope Boniface VIII in which he condemned Emperor Philip IV's embargo on French financial contributions to the church in Rome. In this papal decree Boniface VIII declared that the power of the church exceeded the power of the emperor, so that in effect the emperor in his exercise of civil power became the servant of the pope in the pope's exercise of authority over all Christians everywhere in the Western world (218). The real problem for the long-term ontological identity of the church, however, was that in the High Middle Ages the church had become more and more a juridical entity, a civil power in its own right, rather than primarily a religious institution with focus on effective pastoral ministry to the faithful.

Attempts at Church Reform

Admittedly, throughout the Middle Ages efforts were made by both individuals and groups to return to the ideals of voluntary poverty and simplicity of lifestyle that were preached by Jesus in the gospel narratives. For example, to correct the growing wealth and laxity of life in the monastery, a reform movement was initiated, beginning with the monastery of Cluny in Burgundy, France, in the tenth century. Pope Gregory VII, formerly a monk at Cluny, continued that reform movement in the eleventh century. Bernard of Clairvaux spearheaded the reform movement within monastic life in the twelfth century (220). Likewise among laypeople, resistance to the worldliness of the institutional church began to develop. The Cathars or Albigensians, with their dualistic understanding of the forces of good and evil in civil society, represented an overreaction to clerical power and wealth. But another reform-minded group, the Waldensians, not only criticized the lax lifestyle of the clergy but rebelled against the authority of the pope and bishops on certain doctrinal issues (for example, transubstantiation as explanation for the doctrine of the Eucharist) (221). All these overzealous reform movements were condemned by church authorities at the Fourth Lateran Council in 1215. Moreover, a few years later Pope Gregory IX initiated the Papal Inquisition to prosecute heretics to the faith.

Some of the protest groups, however, like the Franciscans who followed the lifestyle of Francis of Assisi and the Dominicans under the leadership of Dominic Guzman in the early thirteenth century, stayed within the mainstream of the medieval church's life and actively encouraged greater lay participation in spreading the message of the gospel. In the fourteenth century, nevertheless, still other reform movements like the Lollards in England and the Hussites in Bohemia sprung up. They too were denounced and condemned by church authorities (222–28). The failure of the institutional leaders of the church in those centuries to take seriously the concerns of such lay-sponsored reform movements within the church and, as a result, their reluctance to reform the objectionable lifestyle of many clergy (in particular, the extravagant lifestyle of many prelates at the papal court during the Renaissance period), bore a bitter harvest in the Protestant Reformation of the sixteenth century. Even earlier, of course, the papal schism (1378–1417), during which time there were three claimants to the chair of Peter, did considerable damage to the reputation of the papacy in the eyes of ordinary people.

The Protestant Reformation and the Catholic Counter-Reformation

Martin Luther, Augustinian monk and professor of theology at the University of Wittenburg, Germany, proposed in 1517 a public disputation on the legitimacy of selling plenary indulgences to laypeople as remedy for their sins and as an easy way to avoid eternal punishment either for themselves or for relatives and friends (242–43). Luther's view was that only a personal conversion of mind and heart by the penitent could result in genuine forgiveness of sin by God. In 1518, however, Luther was summoned to an imperial diet (assembly) to defend his views on indulgences in debate with Cardinal Cajetan. When he refused to recant, he was excommunicated by Pope Leo X in 1521. At the diet of Worms in 1521, Emperor Charles V ordered that Luther's writings be burned. By this time, of course, the matter of indulgences granted by the pope in return for a sum of money had moved beyond theology into politics with many different groups (local civil rulers, nobility and commoners alike) recommending a change in the way that the church dealt with the people of God (243–46).

The Catholic Counter-Reformation was set in motion by the Council of Trent in northern Italy. The council met in twenty-five sessions between December 1545 and December 1563. Pope Paul III found significant resistance among many cardinals to an ecumenical council at which Protestants would likewise be present. So he eventually collaborated with Emperor Charles V to hold the council without any participation from Protestants and without himself being present; instead, he commissioned papal legates to represent him. Council members aimed at multiple objectives, but these five stand out: (1) to condemn Protestant doctrine and to clarify Catholic Church doctrine on each contested issue; (2) to bring about an internal reformation of church discipline and administration; (3) to make clear that the church is the official interpreter of sacred scripture; (4) to indicate how both faith and good works are needed for salvation; (5) to defend traditional church practices condemned by the Protestants (for example, among others, indulgences, pilgrimages, veneration of relics, devotion to Mary as the Mother of God).[9] The Council of Trent, accordingly, was quite defensive in its response to the challenge of Protestantism, restoring as far as possible the church doctrines and liturgical

---

[9] See also John W. O'Malley, *Trent: What Happened at the Council* (Cambridge, MA: Harvard University Press, 2013), "Appendix A: The Twenty-Five Sessions of the Council of Trent," 279–82, and "Epilogue," 248–75.

practices of the pre-Reformation period. Yet the results of the council were still applauded by the monarchy in France and other Western European countries that remained faithful to the earlier pattern of church life, if only because Protestants were a sufficiently large minority in their midst to present a threat to the stability of their regime.

After the Council of Trent

In the years after the Council of Trent, the Roman Catholic Church primarily focused on the centralization of church structure and organization around the papacy. Prusak states, "As the bulwark of depleted Catholicism, the church of Rome became more and more identified with the universal church, and its bishop viewed almost as a universal bishop" (247). Jesuit theologian Robert Bellarmine, for example, worked out the notion of the church as a "perfect society," that is, a religious institution equipped to function as a civil entity in its own right in much the same way as the civil authorities in the nations of Western Europe at that time conceived themselves to function (248). Thinking of the church in this way was, of course, a virtually inevitable response to a tendency among civil authorities in Western Europe to subordinate the church to the state within their regimes. Moreover, in Italy the church found itself in conflict with the civil government over control of the Papal States, territories in the Italian Peninsula that traditionally belonged to the church rather than to the civil government. So a definitely more authoritarian form of Catholicism took shape in the years before the First Vatican Council in 1870. "Instead of including all of humanity, God's kingdom or reign began to be identified with the Church, in a manner that emphasized the visibility of its hierarchy and authority, and its administration of sacraments as the means to salvation" (250). As a result, the ancient notion of "the sense of the faithful," the role of the entire community of believers in keeping alive the beliefs of the church, was virtually ignored. Admittedly, Johann Adam Möhler, professor of theology at the

University of Tübingen in Germany, continued to emphasize in *Unity in the Church* and other writings that the church in the first place was a community of believers grounded in love rather than in external regulation. But his liberalizing tendencies were effectively countered by the work of Jesuit theologian Joseph Kleutgen at the German College in Rome, who actively supported a revival of Scholastic philosophy and theology, notably that of Thomas Aquinas (252).

Vatican I and Its Aftermath

The First Vatican Council is known for its definition of the personal infallibility of the pope when a serious issue of faith and morals is at stake:

> We teach and define that it is a dogma divinely revealed: that the Roman pontiff, when he speaks *ex cathdra,* that is, when in discharge of the office of Pastor and Doctor of all Christians, by virtue of his supreme apostolic authority he defines a doctrine regarding faith or morals to be held by the Universal Church, by the divine assistance promised him in Blessed Peter, is possessed of that infallibility with which the Divine Redeemer willed that his Church should be endowed for defining doctrine regarding faith or morals: and that therefore such definitions of the Roman pontiff are irreformable of themselves, and not from the consent of the Church.[10]

What the council affirms here, then, is that the pope in settling matters of faith and morals for all Christians enjoys the same inerrancy that Christ intended for the church as a whole. In addition, the pope enjoys that immunity from serious error in his

---

[10] *The Teaching of the Catholic Church,* ed. Karl Rahner, trans. Geoffrey Stevens (Staten Island, NY: Alba House, 1969), 229. See also *Enchiridion Symbolorum Definitionum et Declarationnum de Rebus Fidei et Morum,* ed. Denzinger-Schönmetzer, edition 33 (Herder: Freiburg in Breisgau, 1964), 3074.

own person and not in virtue of a general consensus on the part of his brother bishops and of the faithful around the world. This quite narrow understanding of the infallibility of the church in and through the person of the pope was prompted, as Prusak notes, by threats to the independence of the church on the part of secular states and as a way to counter a revived conciliarist movement in the church whereby the authority of the pope was subject to the authority of an ecumenical council of bishops (255). But it had the unhappy side effect of reducing the role of the bishops around the world to being virtually ambassadors or delegates of the pope even in their own dioceses.

From the standpoint of a systems-oriented approach to church life, the decree on the personal infallibility of the pope was one more sign that the church was moving away from an open-ended approach to life in this world to a closed and relatively deterministic life-system existing in opposition to the outside world. Furthermore, even prior to the council, Pope Pius IX in 1864 published what came to be known as the *Syllabus of Errors,* a document condemning eighty different philosophical positions currently flourishing in Western Europe. Then, after the council in 1910, Pope Pius X decreed that faculty in Catholic seminaries of philosophy and theology and teachers of religious doctrine in parishes must take an oath against modernism, in effect, philosophical and theological positions not in line with the teaching of Thomas Aquinas and his successors. Yet in the same post–Vatican I era, Pope Leo XIII published *Rerum novarum* (1891), a forward-looking papal encyclical on the injustice to workers in the ever-growing industrialized economy of Western Europe and North America. He therein endorsed the right of workers to form labor unions, even as he rejected socialism and unrestricted capitalism. Likewise, he was in favor of a right to private property, provided that one conscientiously set aside surplus funds to assist those in need. This was, moreover, only the first in a series of papal encyclicals on social justice both before and after Vatican II: Pius XI's *Quadragesimo anno* (1931), John XXIII's *Mater et magister* (1961), and John Paul II's *Centesimus annus* (1991).

So the magisterium of the church, in dealing with issues not directly affecting the internal life of the church and the relation of the laity to the clergy, was then and continues to be surprisingly progressive and forward looking in its official teachings.

Events before, during, and after Vatican II

In the years after Vatican I the teaching of theology, above all in seminaries, was dominated by what has been called the manualist approach to the subject. It tended to be regressive in its methodology. That is, it began with the current teaching of the magisterium of the church and sought to find it already in use within the scriptures and the writings of the fathers and doctors of the church. Second, it was conceptualist or grounded in universal concepts rather than in empirically oriented historical and biblical scholarship. Third, it was legalistic, attaching "notes" or qualifications to theological propositions to determine in advance their credibility. Fourth, it was nonliturgical; it did not allow for liturgical rites and the symbolism attached to those rites to be an important locus or source for theology. Finally, it was abstract; it did not appeal to first-person experience of the faith in the writings of theologians like Augustine, mystics like Teresa of Avila and John of the Cross, the *Spiritual Exercises* of Ignatius Loyola, above all his *Rules for the Discernment of Spirits* and so on. Personal experience of the presence and activity of God in one's life was held in suspicion.[11]

But, as already noted, at the end of the nineteenth century Pope Leo XIII published *Rerum novarum*, with its focus on the duty of the church actively to support needed change in the conditions of life and work for the laboring classes in the new industrial era of Western society. Likewise, Joseph Cardijn, a Belgian priest later made a cardinal of the church by Pope

---

[11] Gabriel Flynn and Paul D. Murray, *Ressourcement: A Movement in Twentieth-Century Catholic Scholarship:* Oxford Scholarship Online.

Paul VI, founded the Young Christian Workers movement with its governing principle "see-judge-act." That same methodology significantly influenced Pope John XXIII in the composition of *Mater et magistra* before Vatican II and was a resource for many of the bishops at Vatican II in composing the *Decree on the Apostolate of the Laity* and likewise in the formulation of *Gaudium et spes,* the socially oriented decree on the role of the church in modern society. Furthermore, with their return to the original sources of church tradition in the scriptures and in the writings of the early fathers of the church, a number of German and French theologians before Vatican II had already called into question the virtually exclusive appeal to the writings of Thomas Aquinas and the neo-Scholastic tradition in the church for the exposition of the Catholic faith. So the stage was clearly set for a quiet but intense struggle among different groups for control of the agenda at Vatican II.

As John W. O'Malley comments, there were those who sought significant change in the church's current mode of operation and those who sought to preserve the status quo in the way that the church had functioned since Vatican I or even in large measure since the Council of Trent. Those seeking change were in part historically minded bishops who had been influenced by the return to the sources in scripture and the writings of the fathers of the early church mentioned above, and still other bishops who were familiar with recent work in philosophy and systematic theology and wanted to see these new ideas become part of the church's teaching mission. Those seeking to retain the status quo in the church's mode of operation "fit the stereotype of the proponents of 'Roman theology,' a theology heavily conditioned by canon law, indifferent to the problems raised by historical methods, and often hermeneutically naive."[12] The net result of this division of opinion among the bishops assembled in Rome at Vatican II was that the official decrees of the council were invariably the result of compromise. They could be interpreted

---

[12] John W. O'Malley, *What Happened at Vatican II* (Cambridge, MA: Harvard University Press, 2008), 292–93.

as a basic victory for either side, that is, as vindication of an underlying understanding of the church either as a relatively fixed institutional entity or as a religiously inspired corporate life-system in process of gradual evolution.

Lumen gentium

For example, the *Dogmatic Constitution on the Church (Lumen gentium)* did not begin with a reaffirmation of the hierarchical structure of the church, as in the past, but with the scripturally based endorsement of the church as the people of God, a community of believers, all of whom share in the one priesthood of Christ (LG 9–10).[13] "Through their baptism and confirmation, all are commissioned to that apostolate [the saving mission of the Church] by the Lord himself" (LG 33). Yet in the minds of most of the bishops the apostolate of the laity should be focused on witness to the gospel in the secular world. Only for special reasons are laypeople to be deputed by the bishop "to exercise certain church functions for a spiritual purpose" (LG 33). This is not to deny that the laity are likewise evangelists of the gospel message to the world at large in virtue of their baptism. But their missionary activity should always be exercised under the guidance of the teaching authority of pope and bishops (LG 12).

In composing *Lumen gentium,* the bishops at Vatican II likewise wanted to clarify the proper relation between themselves as an episcopal college and the pope as the Roman pontiff. Each bishop is the authoritative representative of Jesus Christ to the Christians in his diocese. But they all agreed that pope and bishops should never be seen as in conflict with each other but rather as united in the government of the church. Hence, the bishops likewise reasserted their allegiance to Vatican I's declaration of the personal infallibility of the pope when speaking *ex cathedra* on matters of faith and morals. In brief, then,

---

[13] Quotations from Vatican II documents are from Walter M. Abbott, SJ, ed., *Documents of Vatican II* (New York: Guild Press, 1966).

Lumen gentium was unquestionably a compromise document. It can be interpreted both as a vindication of the traditional hierarchical character of the church and as a breakthrough into a new understanding of the church as the people of God or the mystical body of Christ, that is, an ongoing corporate life-system in which everyone plays an important role.

Gaudium et spes

The *Pastoral Constitution on the Church in the Modern World (Gaudium et spes)* is much more clearly a progressive, forward-looking document. As Donald R. Campion notes in his introduction to the document, *Gaudium et spes* is "the only major document to have originated directly from an intervention made on the floor of the conciliar Aula itself," that is, at the close of the first session of the Council on December 4, 1962 (p. 183). That intervention was made by Cardinal Suenens, Archbishop of Mechelen-Brussel, and was later seconded by Cardinal Montini (at that time Archbishop of Milan and later Pope Paul VI), and Cardinal Lecaro, Archbishop of Bologna. None of the preparatory commissions for the Council had seen fit to write a first draft of a pastoral constitution on the church in the modern world as a complement to the doctrinal constitution *(Lumen gentium)*. These three distinguished prelates insisted that such a document must also be written, evaluated by the assembled bishops and published before the end of the council in 1965. The influence of the maxim "see-judge-act," originally employed by Cardinal Joseph Cardijn in his work for the Young Christian Workers in Belgium, was likewise evident in the composition of this document.

The document begins with a surprising statement, given the history of the often guarded relation between the church and the world within the Roman Catholic Church: "The joys and the hopes, the griefs and anxieties of the men of this age, especially those who are poor or in any way afflicted, these too are the joys and hopes, the griefs and anxieties of the followers of Christ. Indeed, nothing genuinely human fails to raise an echo in their hearts" (GS 1). Admittedly, in the conclusion to the document the bishops also claim that they are drawing on "the treasures of Church teaching" (for example, the social encyclicals of Leo XIII to John XXIII and Paul VI) (GS 91). But the style and tone of the document are significantly different from previous papal and conciliar pronouncements.[14] For example, the constitution is addressed "without hesitation, not only to the sons of the Church and to all who invoke the name of Christ, but to the whole of humanity" (GS 2). In that same spirit, there is much greater emphasis in *Gaudium et spes* on freedom of conscience and the right of individuals to make personal choices appropriate to their own life situation than in pre–Vatican II church documents with their customary emphasis on unquestioning obedience to the authority of the church's magisterium on a given issue.

Gaudium et spes is much too long and too detailed to analyze properly here. Hence, I simply offer a quick overview of the two major parts of the Constitution and how they are related to each other. In Part One, the bishops deal in separate chapters with the following topics: the dignity of the human person with emphasis on freedom of conscience; the relation between the individual person and society at large, with special focus on the common good as a shared responsibility; the independence of the social order as an institutional reality in its own right; and the contribution that the church can make both to the prosperity of the individual person and to maintenance of a strong sense of the common good. Here the bishops are seeking common ground not simply with members of the church but with all human beings of good will, as noted above.

In Part Two the bishops are much more clearly addressing fellow members of the church; they are thus much more specific in their teaching on matters of faith and morals. They have, for example, chapters on marriage and the family in which they

---

[14] O'Malley, *What Happened at Vatican II*, 305: "The style of the documents of Vatican II is what at first glance as well as most profoundly sets it apart from all other councils."

stress the importance of conjugal love with sexual intercourse as a normal part of married life. The bishops remain opposed to artificial methods of birth control, but they also fully recognize the need for careful family planning. Second, they recognize the independence of the various forms of human culture from undue influence by the church but stress the importance of the church's teaching based on divine revelation as well as on human reason for influencing the progress of those cultures toward worthwhile goals and values. Third, they lay down guidelines for the regulation of contemporary economic life, for example, endorsement of labor unions to protect the rights of workers vis-à-vis management in the matter of wages, the right of private ownership of property, and fair distribution of profits so as to meet the needs of poor people around the world as well as individual stockholders in multinational corporations. Fourth, the bishops offer guidelines to their church members on the sometimes tangled relation between church and state. The independence of the church from state control and at the same time the noninvolvement of the church in the resolution of contentious political issues must be vigilantly safeguarded. Yet the church should be at the forefront of efforts to maintain peace among nations and thus help to avoid destructive conflict, even open warfare, between nations. Virtually, all these social issues had been analyzed and discussed in previous papal encyclicals, but they are gathered here in *Gaudium et spes* as the final document of the council in order to make clear the church's proper role in contemporary society.

Evaluation and Critique

In retrospect, then, *Lumen gentium* and *Gaudium et spes* were significant milestones in terms of rethinking the traditional mode of operation of the church to deal more directly and effectively with conditions in contemporary society. Granted that the decrees of Vatican II were ambiguously worded by design to get broad approval by the assembled bishops, one can still point to other quite surprising changes, such as approval of the

vernacular language for the celebration of the Eucharist; the
strong recommendation that the priest celebrate the Eucharist
facing the congregation rather than away from it; and the redesign of churches to form a horizontal circle of pews around
the altar rather than being lined up vertically in a succession of
pews stretching back to the front door of the church. Finally,
the unofficial practice of virtually everyone in attendance at
mass receiving communion and the tacitly accepted recognition
of a new freedom of conscience on moral and even doctrinal
issues were clear signs of the significant impact of the decrees
of Vatican II on the lives of the faithful in a way that would
have been unheard of before Vatican II.

But in the view of many conservatively minded clergy and
laypeople to the present moment, all these changes in the traditional mode of operation of the church are seen as danger signs.
For, in their view, the church is becoming much too secular in
its new mode of operation so that continuity with the long-
established tradition of the church seems to be increasingly at
risk. Furthermore, as Bernard Prusak points out, many of the
bishops who were active during the time of the council have
been replaced by bishops who did not share the experience of
Vatican II and who thus have other priorities. "Consequently,
the conciliar solidarity that had developed between pope and
bishops [at Vatican II] has been practically eroded by a resur-
gent solidarity between pope and curia" (302). For example,
Pope John Paul II in his address to the bishops of the United
States in 1992 underscored the notion of communion as being
at the heart of the church's self-understanding (305).[15] But in
a subsequent talk to members of the papal curia he claimed
instead that local churches should be seen as constituted after
the model of the universal church: "One does not belong to
the universal Church in a mediate way, through belonging to
a particular Church, but in an immediate way, even though
entry into and life within the universal Church are necessarily

---

[15] See also *Catholic International* 3 (September 1992), 761–67.

brought about in a particular Church" (307). Such a cautiously worded understanding of the relation between the universal church and individual churches around the world would seem to reflect fear on the part of the pope and Vatican authorities that the term *universal church* could be viewed simply as the sum of all the particular churches rather than as focused on the church in Rome as role model and authoritative source for the existence and activity of the church everywhere. Is there a compromise position available that will be generally acceptable to both liberals and conservatives in the contemporary Roman Catholic Church?

Looking to the Future

On the one hand, my basic hypothesis in this book has been that the church is best understood as an open-ended life-system in active contact with other religious bodies and with all the secular forces at work in contemporary society. On the other hand, how is the church to retain its traditional institutional structure and lines of authority? I believe that the answer to that urgent issue is to be found in a new approach to ministry in the church in which lay members of the parish as well as the clergy and staff are actively involved. My guide here will be Edward Hahnenberg, who published a book on a relational approach to ministry within the local church that allows the parishioners to take a more active role in the life and work of the parish community.[16] Hahnenberg believes that the traditional top-down demarcation between clergy and lay members of the parish is outdated and should be replaced by a new understanding of the parish as the center point and vital source of a variety of ministries to be exercised by different members of the parish community. This approach would begin with the pastor, assistant priests, and deacons (where available), but

---

[16] Edward P. Hahnenberg, *Ministries: A Relational Approach* (New York: Crossroad, 2003).

also extend to full-time and part-time members of the parish staff, and in the end to all parishioners who in different ways would be able to assist in parish ministry both to one another and to the outside world.

So instead of the traditional distinction between ordained and non-ordained members of the parish, Hahnenberg pictures the parish in terms of four concentric circles. The innermost circle is reserved for the ministry of leadership within the parish community as exercised by the pastor and other ordained members of the clergy. The second circle includes full-time professionally trained leaders of important areas of ministry within the community (directors of religious education, youth ministers, the principal and faculty of the parish elementary school, and others). The third circle would be those engaged in part-time ministry within the parish (cantors, lectors, Eucharistic ministers, and such). The outermost circle would be the great bulk of the parishioners, all of whom are commissioned to spread the gospel message to others by reason of their baptism and confirmation.[17]

Hahnenberg also underscores the need for a sacramental or at least a liturgical ceremony for the conferral of ministries within the church. Here too he uses the diagram of four concentric circles constituting church life. The innermost circle, which, as noted above, pertains to the exercise of leadership within the church, is liturgically and sacramentally expressed by the public conferral of holy orders upon candidates for bishop and priest. The second circle, involving leadership within specific areas of ministry within the parish community,

---

[17] Ibid., 127. Hahnenberg freely admits his debt here to Yves Congar, OP, one of the chief advisers to the bishops at Vatican II in composing the *Dogmatic Constitution on the Church* and the *Pastoral Constitution on the Church in the Modern World,* as well as to Thomas F. O'Meara, OP, who used the diagram of concentric circles to explain Congar's views on the role of the laity in the church. See Yves Congar, "Ministères et structuration de l'Église," *Ministères et communion ecclésiale* (Paris: Cerf, 1971), 43–47; Thomas F. O'Meara, *Theology of Ministry*, rev. ed. (New York: Paulist Press, 1999), 183.

should be liturgically symbolized either by public ordination to the diaconate by the bishop or by the official installation of full-time ministers within the parish by the pastor at one of the weekend masses. The third circle, pertaining to those with part-time ministries within the parish, should be solemnized by commissioning ceremonies in which the pastor leads all in attendance at the mass to extend their hands in blessing over the candidate for lector, cantor, or eucharistic minister. Finally, the fourth circle of service to the church involving all the members of the parish is the public conferral of the sacrament of baptism upon adult converts and also infants and their families as part of the weekly Sunday mass instead of, as so often for infants in the past, in a private ceremony on Sunday afternoon after the morning masses. In this way it will be brought home to all the members of the parish that they are a sacramental and liturgical community with everyone witnessing in some way to the spread of the gospel message to one another and to the outside world. Thereby the clergy will take on a new responsibility to the needs of the world as well as to the needs of the church, and the laity in turn will assume a responsibility to one another within the church as well as continue to be a witness to the outside world in terms of spreading the Gospel message.

Evaluation and Critique of Hahnenberg's Proposal

Hahnenberg's notion of the church as ordered communion and ministry fits very nicely with my own understanding of the church as a dynamic life-system. For, in both cases, the church is clearly understood to be both an institutional entity with a relatively stable governing structure of authority and organization and a unity-in-diversity of dynamically inter-related parts or members. Hahnenberg describes this unity-in-diversity within the church as communion; I describe it as a corporate life-system. But the reality thus described is the same. Likewise, like me, Hahnenberg finds the prime analogate for the church as communion or corporate life-system in the Christian doctrine of the Trinity (one God in three Persons).

But Hahnenberg's explanation of the doctrine of the Trinity closely follows the explanation of the doctrine of the Trinity by the Greek Orthodox Bishop John D. Zizioulas, a view that I find questionable. That is, I take issue with Zizioulas's much more speculative approach to the doctrine of the Trinity and its heavily a priori application to the world of finite entities.

To make clear what I have in mind here, I cite the following passage on the Trinity from Zizioulas's book *Communion and Otherness:*

> The first thing that emerges from a study of the doctrine of the Trinity is that otherness is *constitutive* of unity, and not consequent upon it. God is not first one and then three, but simultaneously one and three. His oneness or unity is safeguarded not by the unity of substance, as St. Augustine and other Western theologians have argued, but by the *monarchia* of the Father who is himself one of the Trinity. It is also expressed through the unbreakable *koinonia* that exists between the three Persons, which means that otherness is not a threat to unity but a *sine qua non* condition of it.[18]

Zizioulas thus believes that the classical Greek Orthodox understanding of the Trinity is superior to the traditional Western approach to the doctrine of the Trinity because it finds the unity of God in one of the divine Persons (the Father) rather than in an abstract philosophical concept like substance.

But, as I see it, the ontological unity of the triune God is not in the Father as the first divine Person but in all three divine Persons who are dynamically interrelated to one another as a corporate Reality or divine Community. Zizioulas accounts for the corporate reality of God by referring in the above citation to "the unbreakable *koinonia* that exists between the

---

[18] John D. Zizioulas, *Communion as Otherness: Further Studies in Personhood and the Church* (New York: T and T Clark, 2006), 5.

three persons." Yet, in my view, this is logically inconsistent. Either the ontological unity of the triune God is located in the Person of the Father or in their corporate reality as a divine Community that exercises a unified corporate agency in dealing with creation. It cannot be philosophically grounded in both realities at the same time. Furthermore, Zizioulas contends in another book, *Being as Communion*, that personhood and being in communion are one and the same reality.[19] But, as I see it, personhood (even divine personhood) and being in communion are not strictly interchangeable concepts. One can be quite antisocial in one's dealings with others and still not cease to be a person. Personhood is instead the highest expression of individual subjectivity, that is, being a subject of experience. Not personhood but subjectivity is characteristic of every individual entity that exists.[20] Furthermore, I believe that every individual entity finds its fulfillment in belonging to a socially organized reality, a society or system. But it still exists in its own right simply as a self-constituted momentary subject of experience (in Whiteheadian terms, an actual entity).

I am then uneasy with Zizioulas's approach to the doctrine of the Trinity and indirectly to his understanding of the nature of physical reality, because it is a highly abstract approach to topics that in my judgment should be instead grounded from the bottom up. That is, instead of starting with a speculative theory as to how personhood for the divine Persons is synonymous with being in communion, one should instead start with the de facto empirical reality of subjectivity operative at various levels of existence and activity within the world of nature. Then one should reflect on the relation among mind, brain, and body in the physiology and psychology of human beings. Only afterward should one finally speculate about how divine

---

[19] John D. Zizioulas, *Being as Communion* (Crestwood, NY: St. Vladimir's Seminary Press, 1985), 47.

[20] Alfred North Whitehead, *Process and Reality: An Essay in Cosmology*, corrected ed., ed. David Ray Griffin and Donald W. Sherburne (New York: Free Press, 1978), 18.

personhood and human personhood are both different from and yet in some modest way still analogous to one another.

Fortunately, Hahnenberg's approach to ministry in the church is, for the most part, thoroughly empirical and as a result easy to understand. For, it is far more sensible to undertake a renewal of church life from the bottom up with focus on the local parish instead of proceeding top down via a theory on the inner workings of the Trinity. Then one has a far better chance of getting both liberals and conservatives to work together with a common purpose, namely, to spread the message of the gospel first to one another and then to the civil society in which their parish is located. Likewise, in this way everyone in the parish will begin to feel with Pope Francis "the joy of the Gospel."[21] For me, this idea of the joy of the gospel rings true in the light of my many years of weekend ministry in parishes. Some of these parishes have come alive as a result of the increased participation of ordinary parish members in the work that used to be done exclusively by the pastor and other full-time men and women religious in the parish. One cannot help but notice that the parishioners obviously look forward first to their communal celebration of the Eucharist every week and then to conversation with one another as well as with the celebrant of the mass afterward.

Precisely on this point, however, a new problem exists, given the current priest shortage in the United States and the efforts of bishops officially to deal with this issue in the administration of their dioceses. As William Clark notes in a recent article, the efforts of many bishops to provide pastoral ministry to the faithful, given the fact of fewer and fewer priests, is to close some parishes by executive order and instruct members of those parishes to attend mass and receive other sacraments as

---

[21] Pope Francis, *Evangelii gaudium (The Joy of the Gospel)*: "The joy of the Gospel fills the hearts and lives of all who encounter Jesus. . . . In this exhortation I wish to encourage the Christian faithful to embark upon a new chapter of evangelization marked by this joy, while pointing out new paths for the Church's journey in years to come" (EG 1).

needed in a nearby parish that has more parishioners regularly in attendance every weekend.[22] Admittedly, such a decision on the part of hard-pressed bishops is not inconsistent with the traditional top-down mode of operation of the Catholic Church in the past. But in parishes where the parishioners know one another well and have become familiar with the relational approach to ministry recommended by Hahnenberg, it tends to be a public-relations disaster. Long-term members of the parish feel betrayed by the bishop and his administrative staff and as a result cease going to church altogether, become members of a local Protestant church, or attend mass at the larger Catholic church with little or no enthusiasm or sense of participation in the ongoing activities of the parish.

As I see it, this problematic issue within the Catholic Church in the United States at present is still one more reason to think through more carefully the implications of a systems-ordered understanding of church life and structure that is more oriented to organization from the bottom up than from the top down, as in years past. Pope Francis seems to echo those sentiments in the following citation from his Apostolic Exhortation *Evangelii gaudium* with which I conclude this chapter:

> I dream of a "missionary option," that is, a missionary impulse capable of transforming everything, so that the church's customs, ways of doing things, times and schedules, language and structures can be suitably channeled for the evangelization of today's world rather than for her self-preservation. The renewal of structures demanded by pastoral conversion can only be understood in this light: as part of an effort to make them more mission-oriented, to make ordinary pastoral activity on every level more inclusive and open, to inspire in pastoral workers

---

[22] William A. Clark, SJ, "Nearer the People? Pope Francis and the Crisis of the American Parish," in *American Catholicism in the Twenty-first Century: Crossroads, Crisis, or Renewal*, ed. Benjamin T. Peters and Nicholas Rademacher (Maryknoll, NY: Orbis Books, 2018), 60–71.

a constant desire to go forth and in this way to elicit a
positive response from all those whom Jesus summons to
friendship with himself. (EG 27)

Chapter 5

The Local Parish as Center for Environmental Awareness

In Chapter 4, I reviewed the history of the Catholic Church over the centuries and noted how, under pressure from external forces (e.g., civil authorities, other religious traditions, new developments in the natural sciences), church authorities struggled to maintain the historical integrity and traditional institutional structure of the church. This inward focus on the part of church leaders, however, had the unfortunate consequence of distancing the church as an institution from more active involvement in the ongoing life of the civil society in its midst. From the perspective of a systems-oriented approach to reality, the church was thus inadvertently becoming more and more a closed system—in the words of Cardinal Bellarmine in the years after the Council of Trent, a "perfect society" existing in and for itself in relative independence of the conditions of life in civil society.[1] At the First Vatican Council, in 1870, the assembled bishops formalized the autonomy of the church vis-à-vis civil society with their decree on the personal infallibility of the pope when speaking *ex cathedra* on matters of faith and morals. In an age of great uncertainty in civil society

---

[1] Bernard Prusak, *The Church Unfinished: Ecclesiology through the Centuries* (New York: Paulist Press, 2004), 248.

about what to think and how to proceed, the assurance that the church could never go astray on key moral and doctrinal issues was very reassuring for clergy and laity alike.

But, as I also noted in Chapter 4, uneasiness about the relatively detached role of the church in relation to civil society began to spread among more reflective individuals, above all, those teaching in Catholic seminaries and institutions of higher learning. The *Syllabus of Errors* issued by Pope Pius IX before Vatican I and the oath against modernism decreed by Pope Pius X after the council, for example, had the effect of shutting down discussion of new proposals in philosophy and theology so as not to endanger Catholic orthodoxy. This disquiet about the church's role in public life eventually bore fruit with the unexpected intervention of three prominent cardinals at the first formal session of Vatican II to the effect that a new special decree of the council dealing with the role of the church in the modern world must be composed, discussed, and eventually voted on before the council could be called to a close. That special decree, *Gaudium et spes (Pastoral Constitution on the Church in the Modern World)*, along with other key documents of the council like the *Decree on Ecumenism,* the *Declaration on the Relationship of the Church to Non-Christian Religions,* and especially the *Declaration on Religious Freedom*, all indicated an effort on the part of many, if not most, of the bishops at the council to adopt in varying degrees a more open-ended or receptive approach to new developments in contemporary civil society. Pope Francis's encyclical *On Care for Our Common Home (Laudato si')* represents a continuation of that same more open-ended or exploratory approach to Christian life in the modern world. Citing the socially oriented encyclicals of John XXIII, Paul VI, John Paul II, and Benedict XVI, Pope Francis invites Christians and non-Christians alike to enter into dialogue about still another issue pertinent to life in the modern world, namely, the current state of the environment, "our common home."[2] Widespread exploitation of nature by various individuals, acting either on their own or, more often through their participation in various economic, political, and social systems, is endangering the long-term well-being and even survival of the human species on this earth. In response, Pope Francis agrees with Patriarch Bartholomew, head of the Greek Orthodox Church, that there are ethical and spiritual roots for these environmental issues that "require that we look for solutions not only in technology, but in a change of humanity; otherwise we would be dealing merely with symptoms" (4).

Francis, accordingly, is writing as a spiritual leader, not as a professional economist or environmentalist. The great bulk of his references in the encyclical, for example, are to previous church pronouncements issued by his predecessors as pope or by episcopal conferences in various parts of the world. Yet the encyclical was warmly received by church leaders, both Protestant and Catholic, and by non-Christian religious leaders like the Dalai Lama. Not surprisingly, however, *Laudato si'* was likewise sharply criticized by conservative groups within the Catholic Church and elsewhere who were apprehensive about Francis entering into public dialogue over highly contentious nonreligious issues. In addition, environmental scientists expressed basic approval of the encyclical along with some disappointment that Francis did not acknowledge the related environmental issue of population control and various ways to address it.[3]

But, as the well-known environmentalist Bill McKibben commented, "The empirical data about climate change make

---

[2] Pope Francis, *Laudato si'—On Care for Our Common Home*, June 18, 2015, nos. 1–3. Future paragraph numbers from the document follow quotations in parentheses in the text.

[3] See the editorial "Hope, from the Pope" *Nature* 522 (June 25, 2015): 391.

it clear that the moment is ripe for this encyclical. The long line of brown-robed gurus, of whom Francis is the latest, now marches next to scientists in lab coats; instead of scriptures, the physicists and chemists clutch the latest printout from their computer models, but the two ways of knowing seem to be converging on the same point."[4] That is, further progress in science and technology cannot alone solve all environmental issues. "Pope Francis, in a moment of great crisis, speaks instead to who we could be. As the data suggest, this may be the only option we have left."[5] *Laudato si'* is, then, in the eyes of McKibben and other environmentalists, an important statement on the key issues of climate change and its long-term effects on the environment by the head of an influential organization like the Roman Catholic Church.

I fully agree with McKibben on this point and in this chapter further argue that Francis's main points in the encyclical tacitly reflect an overall systems-oriented or process-oriented approach to the environment and indeed to the God-world relationship that should be set forth in more detail so as to strengthen his overall argument in the encyclical. In addition, in line with the theme of the last chapter on a renewal of church life, I claim in this chapter that Roman Catholics in thus working for improvement of the environment will be contributing to the "missionary option" for church life at the parish level that was recommended by Pope Francis in *Evangelii gaudium*. I likewise use in this chapter the comments of a prominent environmentalist, Holmes Rolston III, both in his ground-breaking book *Environmental Ethics* (1988) and in his updated version of that same book, *A New Environmental Ethics* (2012). As I see it, Rolston is consciously working within a systems-oriented approach to reality much akin to what I presented in Chapter 3.

---

[4] Bill McKibben, "Introduction: On Care for Our Common Home," in *For Our Common Home: Process-Relational Responses to Laudato si'*, ed. John B. Cobb Jr. and Ignacio Castuera (Anoka, MN: Process Century Press, 2015), 8.

[5] Ibid., 9.

Analysis of *Laudato si'*

The encyclical is divided into six chapters. In the first chapter, "What Is Happening to Our Common Home," Francis initially notes that while "change is part of the working of complex systems, the speed with which human activity has developed contrasts with the naturally slow pace of biological evolution. Moreover, the goals of this rapid and constant change are not necessarily geared to the common good or to integral and sustainable human development" (18). In particular, Francis calls attention to the following environmental issues: air pollution, climate change, shortage of safe drinking water, loss of biodiversity as a result of the extinction of species, decline in the quality of human life as a result of overcrowded cities, insufficient public transportation, and increasing global inequality. Finally, with the rapid growth of social media and other forms of digital communication via the Internet, people risk never "learning how to live wisely, to think deeply, and to love generously" (47).

Yet the response to all these changes in the customary pattern of human life on this earth has been pathetically weak. "There are too many special interests, and economic interests easily end up trumping the common good and manipulating information so that their own plans will not be affected" (54). Admittedly, says Pope Francis, there are no fail-safe solutions to combat this slide into environmental degradation. The church itself "has no reason to offer a definitive opinion. She knows that honest debate must be encouraged among experts, while respecting divergent views" (61).

Insights from Sacred Scripture

Yet Francis still puts forth in the second chapter of his encyclical insights derived from the Hebrew and Christian scriptures that, in his mind, should be considered as reflective individuals everywhere rethink how best to proceed in the future. Genesis, for example, teaches that "human life is grounded in three fundamental and closely intertwined relationships: with God, with our neighbor, and with the earth itself" (66). Sin disrupts the relationship with all three. That is, the earth ultimately belongs to God; hence, human beings are expected by God to respect the laws of nature and try to maintain an equilibrium or harmony in dealing with everyone and everything, given that every creature is precious in the eyes of God. "Human beings . . . possess a uniqueness that cannot be fully explained by evolution" (81). But every creature has a purpose within the divine plan of creation. "Peace, justice and the preservation of creation are three absolutely interconnected themes, which cannot be separated and treated individually without once again falling into reductionism" (92). But the claim on the part of individuals to own property and dispose of it as they wish is limited by the perceived common good, especially the rights of the poor and underprivileged to a fair share of nature's resources.

Human Responsibility for Care of the Environment

Armed with these insights from sacred scripture, Francis then turns in chapter three to his analysis of the human roots of the ecological crisis. He first calls attention to the enormous changes in the pattern of human life that have been achieved in the last two centuries through modern technology: "steam engines, railways, the telegraph, electricity, automobiles, airplanes, chemical industries, modern medicine, information technologies and, more recently, the digital revolution, robotics, biotechnologies and nanotechnologies" (102). But he quickly adds that contemporary human beings are not ready to use well this new and unexpected power of technology because technological development "has not been accompanied by a development in human responsibility, values, and conscience" (105). In particular, he claims that contemporary technology is unconsciously governed according to an undifferentiated and one-dimensional paradigm, namely, "the concept of a subject who, using logical and rational procedures, progressively approaches and gains control over an external object. The subject makes every effort to establish the scientific and experimental method, which in itself is already a technique of possession, mastery and transformation" (106).

Background in Early Modern Philosophy

This malfunction in human thinking about self, world, and God has had a long history. As I indicated in Chapter 1, a shift in worldview took place at the start of the seventeenth century in the West from the rational objectivity of the Christian understanding of the God-world relationship in the work of Aquinas and other medieval thinkers to the empirically oriented individual subjectivity of Descartes, Locke, and other philosopher/theologians at that time. This change in perspective on the part of early modern philosophers and theologians was important because it reflected a new awareness of human individuality and uniqueness that was largely overlooked in the cosmologies of the medieval period. As time went on, however, it became clear to reflective individuals that knowledge based on personal experience is perspectival and thus offers no strict guarantee that one's judgment about self, world, and God is correct. Hence, one must find a new starting point for a realistic and objective understanding of reality.

Kant's Copernican Revolution

Immanuel Kant provided that new starting point with his controversial proposal that in the act of cognition the human mind does not conform to physical reality but that physical reality conforms to the workings of the human mind as it shapes the data of sense experience in line with an a priori set of principles. Kant mistakenly believed that his conceptual scheme was grounded in the traditional logical categories originally set forth by Aristotle and thus would work the same way in the act of cognition for every human being. New discoveries in the rapidly developing sciences of psychology and cultural anthropology, however, made clear that this was not the case.

Human beings differ broadly in their understanding of self, world, and God. But at the same time, Kant's hypothesis seemed to confirm the way that natural scientists were already experimenting with empirical data in their search for the laws of nature. That is, in their minds the world of nature can and should be understood and controlled for human purposes in and through empirical observation of nature's workings, followed by the formulation of a mathematically based hypothesis that can be tested empirically by oneself and others working in the same field of scientific research.

This new way to deal with and control for human purposes the world of nature was marvelously successfully in physics, chemistry, biology, and other scientific disciplines. But, as Pope Francis notes, this methodological breakthrough has thus far not been accompanied by a corresponding "development in human responsibility, values, and conscience" (105). So, although very valuable in itself as a tool for successful research into the workings of physical reality, the limitations of a purely empirical and quantitatively based analysis of reality for full understanding of self, world, and God have to be acknowledged. A different approach to the natural world, a new scientific methodology that focuses on a more relational and holistic understanding of the situation at hand, must be developed so that contemporary human beings can make more balanced judgments on the goals and values to be pursued in contemporary society.

Whitehead's Organismic Approach to Reality

As explained in Chapter 2, Alfred North Whitehead saw clearly the mental trap into which early modern natural scientists had fallen with their focus on a fixed, purely quantitative analysis of physical reality. As Whitehead saw it, nature is alive, not dead. It is a historical process, an open-ended system with dynamically interrelated components. Admittedly, most natural scientists still resist Whitehead's proposal on the grounds that they see few if any signs of spontaneous activity among atoms and molecules as the basic components of physical reality. But there are distinct advantages in thinking of the ultimate units of physical reality as alive and responsive to one another. For, in this way there is far less danger of putting one's confidence in an abstract rational scheme rather than in close analysis of the spontaneity and relative unpredictability of the workings of nature.

Likewise, the danger of what Pope Francis in *Laudato si'* calls "the technocratic paradigm" (109) is greatly reduced. The technocratic paradigm is based on what the Jewish philosopher Martin Buber calls an "I-It" as opposed to an "I-Thou" relation.[6] That is, one treats all the other creatures of this world, both human and non-human, as inanimate things rather than as subjects of experience like oneself. In this way one can systematically exploit all these other entities for one's own purposes, and in the achievement of one's self-centered goals and values (see 109). But, if the ultimate constituents of reality are subjects of experience like oneself, one cannot (or at least should not) employ the technocratic paradigm to exploit them for the sake of personal advantage.

Pope Francis, of course, was writing from the perspective of a pastor rather than that of a philosopher of science like Whitehead. But, like Whitehead, he recognizes the danger of "a reductionism which affects every aspect of human and social life" (107). Admittedly, in chapter three of *Laudato si'* he is somewhat pessimistic about the chances of effectively counteracting the continued broad use of the technocratic paradigm in contemporary society. But he still maintains hope in the possibility of a new way of looking at things, "a way of thinking, policies, an educational program, a lifestyle and a spirituality which together generate resistance to the assault of the technocratic paradigm" (111). Furthermore, he seems to find this counterbalance to the technocratic paradigm in the notion of an "integral ecology" in chapter four.

---

[6] Martin Buber, *I and Thou*, trans. Walter Kaufmann (New York: Scribner's, 1970), 54.

Outline of an Integral Ecology

But what is an integral ecology? Is it a uniform reality in which a single system (for example, the economic system) incorporates all the other systems (for example, interpersonal, political, and social) into its own specialized mode of operation? Or is it a more diversified reality in which a great number of different systems are component parts or members? That is, economics, politics, culture, and others all have something to say about environmental issues, but none of them has a controlling influence on what policies will be agreed and acted upon. Which understanding of an integral ecology did Francis have in mind? My conclusion is that he moved in the direction of a more diversified, process-oriented understanding of an integral ecology but never said so directly. He simply illustrated what he meant with multiple practical examples. For example, he distinguishes among environmental, economic, and social ecologies, but then he adds: "We are faced not with two separate crises, one environmental and the other social, but rather with one complex crisis which is both social and environmental" (139). Furthermore, "When we speak of the 'environment,' what we really mean is a relationship between nature and the society which lives in it. Nature cannot be regarded as something separate from ourselves or as a mere setting in which we live. We are part of nature, included in it and thus in constant interaction with it" (139). Finally, "We take these systems into account not only to determine how best to use them, but also because they have an intrinsic value independent of their usefulness. Each organism, as a creature of God, is good and admirable in itself; the same is true of the harmonious ensemble of organisms existing in a defined space and functioning as a system" (140). Taken together, these statements flesh out what he means by an integral ecology, one based on the coordination of sub-systems within a still higher-order system rather than the subordination of all other systems to a single system with its own limited goals and values (for example, the technocratic paradigm for Pope Francis).

Community Involvement from the Bottom Up

Pope Francis also makes reference to the pattern of life in local communities around the world. "Attempts to resolve all problems through uniform regulations or technical interventions can lead to overlooking the complexities of local problems which demand the active participation of all members of the community" (144). Note how Francis here subtly calls attention to the priority of organization from the bottom up as opposed to organization from the top down in the life of a local community. Both forms of organization are needed to deal with the details of community life. But bottom-up organization better lends itself to change and innovation in the pattern of life within a community as its members respond to unexpected changes among themselves and in relation to the external environment. For example, within overcrowded urban centers—where a sense of social anonymity can readily develop and as a result a thinly disguised segregation on the basis of race, class, wealth, and other cultural factors can spawn antisocial behavior and violence—only a renewed sense of community life can bring people together again. It is then important that "the different parts of a city be well integrated and that those who live there have a sense of the whole, rather than being confined to one neighborhood and failing to see the larger city as space which they share with others" (151). City planners and others involved in urban renewal should likewise keep this need for sustained interaction in mind as they set up common recreational areas and redesign the transportation system of the urban complex.

"Underlying the principle of the common good is respect for the human person as such, endowed with basic and inalienable rights ordered to his or her integral development. It has also to do with the overall welfare of society and the development of a variety of intermediate groups, applying the principle of subsidiarity" (157). These intermediate groups, both formal and informal in their mode of operation, are indispensable if one is to safeguard bottom-up as well as top-down organization in

bringing about a sense of the common good that is representative of the interests of all members of the community and thus
does not just cater to the lifestyle of more privileged groups
within the community. Finally, in gauging the common good,
one likewise has to think of what the current generation will
in due time be handing on to future generations by way of a
sustainable environment. Here, too, a short-term gain in quality of life for relatively affluent groups of people here and now
should not be gained at the price of a much reduced quality of
life for rich and poor alike in future generations (see 159–60).

Yet one should not just complain about an unjust social
order and then do nothing about it. For, as Peter Berger and
Thomas Luckmann point out in *The Social Construction of
Reality*, human beings over time create the structures of society within which they live. Hence, human beings are also
responsible for collectively changing those structures when they
longer serve the common good.[7] But this cannot be done by
individuals acting alone; it must be done collectively through
organization for social change. Chapter four of *Laudato si'*,
accordingly, is dedicated to laying out "major paths of dialogue which can help us escape the spiral of [environmental]
self-destruction which currently engulfs us" (163). A global
consensus is essential for confronting the deeper problems,
which cannot be resolved by unilateral actions on the part of
individual countries (see 164).[8]

Unfortunately, "recent World Summits on the environment have not lived up to expectations because, due to lack
of political will, they were unable to reach truly meaningful
and effective global agreements on the environment" (166).

---

[7] Peter L. Berger and Thomas Luckmann, *The Social Construction of Reality: A Treatise in the Sociology of Knowledge* (New York:
Doubleday, 1966), 49–50: "Social order exists only as a product of
human activity. . . . Both in its genesis (social order is the result of past
human activity) and its existence in any instant of time (social order
exists only and insofar as human activity continues to produce it) it
is a human product."

[8] Ibid.

Countries are placing their national interests above the global common good. For example, countries that are already heavily industrialized and have contributed most to global pollution should in justice bear greater financial responsibility for reducing emissions than countries who have only recently undergone industrialization and are still in the process of creating a sustainable economy. Furthermore, solving the problem of global pollution by nations "buying and selling 'carbon credits'" does not really reduce global pollution but instead provides an excuse for relatively affluent countries to continue polluting the environment in much the same way as in the past (171). Sadly, the viability of the United Nations as an international organization for dealing with serious environmental problems seems to be weakening rather than getting stronger in the face of transnational economic and political forces that more directly impact upon the way that people around the world live (see 169).

At the same time, equitable solutions of environmental issues cannot be simply left up to national and local political bodies. For, on the one hand, "global regulatory norms are needed to impose obligations and prevent unacceptable actions when, for example, powerful companies find ways to dump contaminated waste offshore or to set up polluting industries in other countries" (173). But, on the other hand, national and local bodies for enforcement of environmental regulations are themselves often too weak or subject to corruption when appropriate measures to correct environmental abuse are urgently needed.

Yet all is not lost. "In some places, cooperatives are being developed to exploit renewable sources of energy which ensure local self-sufficiency and even the sale of surplus energy" (179). Even more important, local cooperatives engender "a greater sense of responsibility, a strong sense of community, readiness to protect others, a spirit of creativity and a deep love for the land" (179). From the perspective of the systems-oriented approach to reality that I have set forth in previous chapters of this book, this is to be expected. As Alfred North Whitehead (in *Process and Reality*) and Terrence Deacon (in *Incomplete Nature*) argued, organization within natural systems does not for the most part work top down but arises from the dynamic interrelationship of their constituents (both human and non-human) from moment to moment. For, as Pope Francis notes, political activity on the local level can be simultaneously effective on multiple fronts, for example, "modifying consumption, developing an economy of waste disposal and recycling, protecting certain species and planning a diversified agriculture and the rotation of crops" (180). The local level within the church, of course, is the parish, provided that the pastor, lay staff, and parishioners are motivated to work together for environmental change.

Recommendations of Pope Francis

Throughout chapter five Francis offers "Lines of Approach and Action" for dealing with environmental issues. Here too he is thinking of making changes more from the bottom up than from the top down, that is, from local people engaged in dialogue with one another rather than from bureaucracies that are often corrupted by external economic and political interests. For example, transparency in decision making is virtually guaranteed if local people "are concerned about their own future and that of their children, and can consider goals transcending immediate economic interest" (183). Admittedly, environmental issues are often quite complicated and thus require the input of trained professionals. But even in that case the burden of proof lies with the experts that the various changes in dealing with the environment that they propose "will not cause serious harm to the environment or to those who inhabit it" (186). In similar fashion Francis suggests that "the time has come to accept decreased growth in some parts of the world, in order to provide resources for other places to experience healthy growth" (193). But that is unlikely to happen unless and until local interests are also involved in decision making about further economic growth. "In a word, businesses profit by calculating and paying only a fraction of the cost involved. Yet only when 'the economic and social costs of using up shared environmental resources are recognized with transparency and fully borne by those who incur them, not by other peoples or future generations,' can these actions be considered ethical" (195). Francis also recommends dialogue between religion and science, to be undertaken not simply by theologians and natural scientists in professional convocations, but much more informally by the believers of the various world religions as they discuss with one another in local settings how best "to live in a way consonant with their faith and not to contradict it by their actions" (200).

The sixth and last chapter of *Laudato si'* is entitled "Ecological Education and Spirituality." Here, too, Francis is thinking in terms of bottom-up rather than top-down organization in producing healthy change in people's attitude toward the environment. He recommends, for example, that Christians adopt a new lifestyle not governed by compulsive buying and spending. For an all-pervasive consumerist mentality leads to social unrest and even overt violence when one is not among the chosen few in society who have the financial means to satisfy their every whim. At the same time, ordinary people in local settings have the power collectively to boycott the sale of certain products (in the first place, nonessentials like luxury items) and thereby force corporations to change their marketing policies, business practices, and patterns of production that are ultimately harmful to both their employees and the external environment. "Disinterested concern for others, and the rejection of every form of self-centeredness and self-absorption, are essential if we truly wish to care for our brothers and sisters and for the natural environment" (208).

Francis likewise proposes new goals for environmental education. "Whereas in the beginning it was mainly centered on scientific information, consciousness-raising and the prevention of environmental risks, it tends now to include a critique of the 'myths' of a modernity grounded in a utilitarian mindset (individualism, unlimited progress, competition, consumerism, the unregulated market)" (210). The ongoing cultivation of environmentally sensitive habits in dealing with the environment is thus far more important than simply up-to-date information on the environment or even the official enactment of new environmental regulations. Much more to the point are the day-to-day decisions of individuals in their local neighborhoods by "avoiding the use of plastic and paper, reducing water consumption, separating refuse, cooking only what can reasonably be consumed, showing care for other living beings, using public transport or car-pooling, planting trees, turning off unnecessary lights, or any number of other practices" (211). For this and other reasons, concludes Francis, "All Christian communities have an important role to play in ecological education" (214).

A Down-to-Earth Ecological Spirituality

Francis concludes *Laudato si'* with "a few suggestions for an ecological spirituality grounded in the convictions of our faith, since the teachings of the Gospel have direct consequences for our way of thinking, feeling and living" (216). For example, Christians believe that God created the world, "writing into it an order and a dynamism that no human beings have a right to ignore" (221). Likewise, Christ became incarnate in this world and in the gospel text reassures his listeners that his Father in heaven cares for every creature in this world. "Are not five sparrows sold for two pennies? Yet not one of them is forgotten in God's sight" (Luke 12:6). Human beings then have a responsibility to care for the nonhuman creatures of this world and to cultivate a more peaceful attitude toward one another and the natural world within which one lives. "Christian spirituality proposes a growth marked by moderation and the capacity to be happy with little. It is a return to that simplicity which allows us to stop and appreciate the small things, to be grateful for the opportunities which life affords us, to be spiritually detached from what we possess, and not to succumb to sadness for what we lack" (222). Francis later adds: "Love, overflowing with small gestures of mutual care, is also civic and political, and it makes itself felt in every action that seeks to build a better world" (231). One does not have to become directly involved in the political life of one's civic community. Besides the local parish, there are multiple other organizations that try to promote the common good and protect the environment.[9] In this way, "a community can break out of the indifference [to life around itself] induced by consumerism" (232).

Yet participation of Christians in the sacramental life of the church is still a privileged way to feel a bondedness and intimacy with God, one another, and the entire world of creation. Especially in celebrating together the Eucharist, Christians are engaged in an act of cosmic love. "Because even when it is celebrated on the humble altar of a country church, the Eucharist is always in some way celebrated on the altar of the world" (236).[10] Making reference to the life of the three divine Persons, Francis notes: "The divine Persons are subsistent relations, and the world, created according to the divine model, is a web of relationships. . . . Everything is interconnected, and this invites us to develop a spirituality of that global solidarity which flows from the mystery of the Trinity" (240).

Overall Evaluation of Laudato si'

In retrospect, then, *Laudato si'* is both much akin to a long line of socially oriented papal encyclicals, beginning with Pope Leo XII's encyclical *Rerum novarum* in 1891, and yet different from the others in that it seems to be devoted to a study of problems within the existing social order from a more

---

[9] In a subsequent papal exhortation, *Amoris laetitia*, Pope Francis refers to the family as equivalently the "front-line" in the ongoing life of the church. Hence, environmental awareness should begin with the family but not end there. Cf. *The Joy of Love: On Love in the Family* (Paulist Press: New York, 2016).

[10] This quotation within the encyclical is from an encyclical letter of Pope John Paul II (*Ecclesia de Eucharistia* [April 17, 2003]). Cf. Teilhard de Chardin, "Mass on the World," *Hymn of the Universe* (New York: Harper and Row, 1961).

evolutionary and systems-oriented approach. That is, Pope Francis spends a fair amount of time in the encyclical analyzing the interplay of complex physical systems in their collective impact upon the physical environment rather than simply on the interactions of individual human beings here and now in dealing with problematic ethical issues in their personal lives. This is, of course, not to deny the responsibility of individuals in setting up and then maintaining or, for good reason, changing the various social systems within which they live.[11] But this systems-oriented approach to reality does challenge the feeling of apathy and sense of hopelessness that human beings often experience in contemplating significant changes in the social order. For, it is easy to complain that the prevailing social order or "system" is bigger than themselves as individuals. Furthermore, if they try to change it and fail, they might instead become victims of the system in a way that far surpasses what they hitherto have negatively experienced for themselves and their families. So their complicity in, or at least compliance with, the perpetuation of an unjust social system ends up as a sin of omission rather than commission, failure to do what is right rather than doing something clearly wrong.

Hence, in addressing the disastrous impact of the technocratic paradigm on contemporary human life rather than simply urging individuals to stop harming or violating the rights of their neighbor on a person-to-person basis, Francis in *Laudato si'* seems to be moving away from the traditional mindset of classical philosophy and theology with its focus on individual human beings and their relations with one another in terms of general moral principles to a more systems-oriented approach to reality in which one needs the advice of professionals in the pertinent natural and social sciences in order to comprehend and adequately deal with the situation at hand. As far as I know, Francis consulted broadly with experts in many fields other than philosophy and theology before composing

---

[11] See Berger and Luckmann, *The Social Construction of Reality*, 49–50.

Laudato si', and the encyclical as a result was warmly received and highly praised by many more people than would otherwise be the case.

Analysis of Environmental Issues by Holmes Rolston III

I now turn to the work of a prominent philosopher of science who has been for many years involved with environmental issues, namely, Holmes Rolston III. In the 1970s Rolston was already active in promoting the notion of an environmental ethics.[12] In 1988 he published a major work, *Environmental Ethics*, with a focus on the intrinsic value of everything that exists within the natural world and the responsibility of human beings to treat nonhuman entities as worthy of respect in their own right apart from their usefulness to satisfy the needs and desires of human beings.[13] Subsequently, Rolston published eight other books on environmental issues and the dialogue between religion and science. In my overview I focus on his 2012 book *A New Environmental Ethics: The Next Millennium for Life on Earth*.[14] Therein, after an introductory chapter on the history of the environmental movement, he devotes separate chapters to human beings, animals, organisms (insects and plants), species, and ecosystems. The range of his inquiry makes clear that an environmental ethic should not be limited to the value of the environment for human beings but must be expanded to include all forms of life, even ecosystems and the cosmic process as a whole. In like manner, Pope Francis

---

[12] Holmes Rolston III, "Is There an Ecological Ethic?" *Ethics: An International Journal of Social and Political Philosophy* 85 (1975): 93–109.

[13] Holmes Rolston III, *Environmental Ethics: Duties to and Values in the Natural World* (Philadelphia: Temple University Press, 1988).

[14] Holmes Rolston III, *A New Environmental Ethics: The Next Millennium for Life on Earth* (New York: Routledge, 2012). Page numbers for quotations from this book appear in parenthesis in the text.

in describing the mystery of the universe in *Laudato si'* said: "Every creature is thus the object of the Father's tenderness, who gives it its place in the world. Even the fleeting life of the least of beings is the object of his love, and in its few seconds of existence, God enfolds it with his affection" (77). Yet Pope Francis was here echoing the sentiments of Francis of Assisi in seeing the nonhuman creatures as quasi-sacramental signs of the presence of God to human beings. Rolston, as a philosopher of science, wants to ground the value of nonhuman creation as well as the value of human beings in the workings of the cosmic process as an objective reality in its own right.

Effects of Environmental Change on Human Beings

With reference to the effect of environmental change on human beings, Rolston first calls attention to the notion of sustainable development coming out of the United Nations Conference on Environment and Development in 1992. Sustainable development "is an orienting concept that is at once directed and encompassing, a coalition-level policy that sets aspirations, thresholds, and allows pluralist strategies for their accomplishment" (36–37). But value judgments on what is meant by sustainable development still have to be made that are beyond the competence of either economists or environmentalists alone. Only in conjunction with philosophers (and theologians like Pope Francis) can one find a balance between legitimate growth of the economy and maintaining a healthy environment for all the inhabitants of the earth. The governing presupposition of some scientists that "man is the measure of all things,"[15] is dangerous in Rolston's view: "The decisions we and our children make are going to have much more influence over the shape of evolution in the foreseeable future than physical events" (44). Humans live in both nature and culture, although increasingly more in culture as shaped by human needs and desires than in

---

[15] A statement attributed to the ancient Greek philosopher Protagoras (481–411 BCE).

nature in a wilderness state such as is found in national and state parks in the United States. But, at the same time, "a really exciting difference between humans and non-humans is that, while animals and plants can count (defend) only their own lives, with their offspring and kind, humans can count (defend) life and even nonlife with vision of greater scope" (59). Human altruism toward others thus extends beyond the claims of other human beings to the simultaneously valid claims of nonhumans, even ecosystems, species, and landscapes.

Effects on Animals

Rolston focuses next on the intrinsic value of animals, both domesticated and living in the wild, and the different ways in which human beings relate to them. "Animals are value-able, able to value things in their world, their own lives intrinsically and their resources instrumentally" (63). Accordingly, animals, like human beings, prize their own individuality or subjectivity. On this point, however, animal-rights advocates and environmentalists take different approaches to the welfare of individual animals. For, saving the life of individual animals, above all, those living in the wild, may in fact be bad for the long-term survival of the species. Natural selection must be allowed to work even if it inevitably involves pain and an early death for defective members of a given species.

There should, moreover, be no sense of guilt among human beings in raising animals for food consumption, writes Rolston: "Keep and eat animals, but show as much respect as you can for their welfare; treat them as humanely as possible, given that beef cows are raised to be eaten. Similarly, with pigs, chickens, turkeys, and other domestic food animals" (77). Factory farming of animals is, of course, a different story since it reduces animals simply to marketable objects of consumption. In addition, problems exist for both factory owners and local inhabitants in terms of proper disposal of animal waste. As for the morality of zoos, that is, keeping animals caged for human display, there are certainly educational benefits, especially for children, in seeing wild animals "up close," but at the same time animals are not allowed to roam freely as they would in their natural environment. So "the ethics of keeping animals in zoos remains confused, and there seem to be no satisfactory solutions on the horizon" (86). Finally, using animals for scientific research is legitimate, but such research must be regulated in line with the Animal Welfare Act passed by the US Congress in 1966, notes Rolston (86). Experimenting on primates, as a result, has been almost entirely stopped. At the same time, a new drug is seldom provided for human use without prior testing on non-primates. Yet here too concern for pain to the animal undergoing such tests has become much more common, partly out of genuine concern for the animal but also out of fear of adverse publicity and loss of institutional permission to continue research on a new drug.

Effects on Insects and Plants

Rolston begins the next chapter of his book with a wry comment about the place of human beings and other sentient animals in the overall population of living things in this world. "The sentient animals form only a minuscule fraction of the living organisms on Earth. Over 96% of species are invertebrates [insects] or plants" (93). Furthermore, "These 'lower organisms' can do without us, but we 'higher humans' cannot do without them" (95). To stay alive, we eat them or we eat other animals (cows, pigs, chickens, fish) that feed on them. In addition, insects pollinate the plants that we eat. But, one may object, are not such lower-level organisms without any sense of feeling? Rolston replies: "A plant is not an experiencing subject, but neither is it an inanimate object, like a stone. . . . Plants are quite alive" (96). While plants do not have goals in life like human beings and other higher-order animal species, they still follow a plan in their growth, reproduction, and repair of wounds. That plan is coded and stored in their genes as information vital to their proper growth and ultimate survival (97).

For example, genes are mini-organisms that are surprisingly adaptive in response to their ever-changing physical environment. "Genes have substantial solution-generating capacities. Though not deliberated in the conscious sense, the process is cognitive, or cybernetic. A genome [an organism's set of DNA molecules] has an array of sophisticated enzymes to cut, splice, digest, rearrange, mutate, reiterate, edit, correct, translocate, invert and truncate particular gene sequences" (103).

Rolston also talks about exotic (literally, "out of place") plants that have invaded a landscape other than the one in which they originated and then asks whether these plants should be rooted out like weeds or whether they should be allowed to grow so as to enhance biodiversity. He concludes with most environmentalists that these invasive forms of plant life should be weeded out since they endanger the integrity and ongoing continuity of the ecosystems that they invade. Rolston accents the priority of biocentrism over anthropocentrism. "Humans are absolutely dependent on other forms of life, but they do not depend on us. . . . Plants can photosynthesize, as animals cannot; and all animals, humans included, depend on this photosynthesis" (111). Yet he is not in favor of "biocentric egalitarianism," according to which all living things have the same inherent worth or value. "All species show preference to their own species. But the good obtained must be proportionate to the harm caused" (112). Hence, human beings must be careful to keep legitimate satisfaction of their basic needs within bounds and respect the interests, if not the legal rights, of other species to exist and flourish.

Along the same lines, Rolston takes note of the view held by many philosophers and humanists that plants and values have no objective value in and for themselves but have only instrumental value vis-à-vis the needs and desires of human beings. But he himself sides with environmentalists and biologists that "there is value wherever there is positive creativity" (122). Creativity is present in individual organisms as they struggle to exist in an unexpectedly hostile environment and in species that sustain a biological identity over time. "What's going on is life persisting in the midst of its perpetual perishing. Humans ought to respect such life" (122).

Rolston's Objection to Reductive Materialism

Rolston is challenging here the reductive materialism of some natural scientists in which organic life (as opposed to inanimate matter) is either nonexistent (ultimately an illusion) or is emergent out of nonliving or material components under specified conditions (for example, the theory for the emergence of life and mind out of material constituents in the philosophy of Terrence Deacon as described in Chapter 3). But Rolston is not for that same reason a disciple of Alfred North Whitehead with the latter's presupposition that the ultimate constituents of physical reality are mini-organisms, that is, momentary self-constituting subjects of experience (actual entities). For, as a natural scientist, he instead claims that there is no verifiable empirical evidence for the existence and activity of momentary self-constituting subjects of experience as the ultimate constituents of everything else that exists.

As already mentioned in Chapter 2, however, Whitehead would counter-argue that there is de facto empirical verification of the existence of momentary self-constituting subjects of experience in rapid succession if one attends to the ongoing flow of events within one's self-consciousness. No moment of consciousness is ever precisely the same as its predecessor. At every moment one is a new subject of experience dealing with new content from the outside world. One's personal identity is thus not a fixed reality but reconstituted over and over again by an ongoing flow of perceived events with the same "common element of form" or governing structure. Whitehead then argues that our human self-consciousness is the only empirical reality that we can understand, so to speak, from "the inside." Hence, it is the best indicator of how de facto everything else in the cosmic process works. In any case, if Rolston could be persuaded to follow the lead of Whitehead here, he could make a much stronger rational argument that life in all its forms is marked by creativity and, in particular, that genes, the building blocks of life, are not inanimate carriers of genetic information but alive and smart, that is, responsive to changes both in their relations to one another and in the external environment.[16]

Objective Reality of Individual Species and Ecosystems

In the next two chapters of his book Rolston defends the objective reality of species and ecosystems over against those who would consider these terms as purely mental constructs for human organization of physical reality. A species has an objective reality in that is "a specific form of life historically maintained over generations for thousands of years" (127). In fact, a species "is more real, more value-able than the individual, necessary though individuals are for the continuance of this lineage" (127). In that sense, species are the real units of evolution, because the species preserve adaptations originally made by individuals. Species should be preserved from extinction, not simply because they are valuable in different ways for human well-being and survival, but in and for themselves as specific life-forms. "To kill a particular animal is to stop a life of a few years or decades, while other lives of such kind continue unabated; to superkill [render extinct] a particular species is to shut down a story of many millennia, and leave no future possibilities" (135). Admittedly, 98 percent of the species that have inhabited the earth are extinct. But there is

---

[16] See Evelyn Fox Keller, *The Century of the Gene* (Cambridge, MA: Harvard University Press, 2000), 147: "Genes have had a glorious run in the twentieth century, and they have inspired incomparable and astonishing advances in our understanding of living systems. Indeed, they have carried us to the edge of a new era in biology, one that holds out the promise of even more astonishing advances. But these very advances will necessitate the introduction of other concepts, other terms, and other ways of thinking about biological organization, thereby inevitably loosening the grip that genes have had on the imagination of life-scientists these many decades."

a major difference between natural and humanly generated extinction of species. In natural extinction one species disappears but its extinction enables another species to take its place (for example, humans and other mammals taking the place of dinosaurs). Humanly caused extinctions simply stop natural speciation and thereby can have a significantly negative effect on habitats and even entire ecosystems. "A species is what it is where it is. Particular species may not be essential in the sense that the ecosystem can survive the loss of individual species. But habitats are essential to species, and an endangered species often means an endangered habitat" (146).

With respect to ecosystems, says Rolston, some are constant with little or no change; others are persistent, lasting a long time; still others are elastic, returning rapidly to a former state after perturbation (160). Whether human beings have duties with respect to the ecosystem in which they live is a matter of debate among both scientists and ethicists. Some say that ecosystems lack central organization and are thus nothing more than a loose collection of externally related parts or members. Others argue that an ecosystem is "a comprehensive, complex, fertile order just because it integrates (with some openness) the know-how of many diverse organisms and species. It is not an order built on the achievement of any one kind of thing" (167). Value lies in processes as well as in products. Here, too, Rolston's basic argument would be strengthened if he explicitly employed a systems-oriented approach to reality such as I set forth in Chapter 3. That is, physical reality is constituted not by a relatively fixed hierarchy of individual entities as in classical metaphysics, but by a temporally ordered succession of dynamically interrelated systems, each with its own integrity but finding its further meaning and value in the higher-order system(s) of which it is already or soon will be a constituent part or member.

There is, of course, a tension between a sustainable ecology and classical economic theory. Economists, notes Rolston, heavily base their thinking on cost-benefit analysis: "The goal is more goods and services available to more people than ever before: more intelligent exploitation of nature" (169). Ecologically oriented economists, on the contrary, find that the goal of giving people more and more goods and services, however humane it may seem at the time, drives an escalating degradation of the natural environment; undermines ecosystem services; reduces biodiversity; pollutes air, water, and soil; and makes the rich richer and the poor poorer (169). Hence, a compromise between the goals and values of economists and the goals and values of environmentalists is urgently needed. Rolston recommends government protection of wilderness areas where people living in overcrowded cities can experience nature firsthand. But, even more important, he favors deliberate ecosystem management that protects natural values as well as one that supports cultural values. Ecosystem management needs a focus on bioregions, "a place defined by its life forms, its topography, and its biota, rather than by human dictates" (189). Landscape architects and county commissioners should be encouraged to think along the same lines in planning new urban neighborhoods.

Earth as a Historical Process

In the final chapter of his book Rolston focuses his attention on the earth as a planet with a past, present, and future. "The Earth story is the larger history to which we also belong, along with the myriads of creatures great and small. . . . Our identity is cultural, culturally specific, yes, but our identity is also flesh and blood, emplaced in the array of metabolic processes in which we are set" (220). Hence, attention should be given to the liabilities as well as the strengths of global capitalism. "Maximizing profits in a free-trade world may produce many benefits. But business that is so minded has no evident concern for biodiversity, for preserving scenic beauty on landscapes, or even for local sustainability—if it can cut and run to another country at will" (200). Human population control is also an increasingly urgent issue for the future of planet earth. "Currently, about 80 million persons are added to Earth's population each year" (207). Further economic development is clearly needed to feed, clothe, and house all these newcomers to the human population, but such development must be carefully managed vis-à-vis environmental factors so as not to risk deforestation, soil loss, biodiversity loss, and pollution. Rolston believes that the focus for population control should not be on increased economic development or on mandatory birth control but on the education of women. "When women have sufficient education, they have knowledge and power enough to make informed decisions about reproduction, less dependence on their men for support, now having workplace skills themselves, and better overall health. . . .With smarter mothers, population growth declines" (210).

Final Thoughts

With respect to the overall issue of global warming, Rolston claims that it may be almost "too hot to handle." It is such a complex issue (climatological, economic, political, and ultimately moral) (210). For example, rich countries should realistically pay more than poor countries to bear the heavy costs of effective climate change. "This is partly because they are able to, partly because they have enjoyed the benefits of pollution more. But also it is because if the poor [countries] are to develop, they must be allowed some interim license to pollute in the period when they are developing but are as yet too poor to be able to afford high-cost, low-polluting technologies" (214). Yet, difficult as it may be to deal with fairly, climate change cannot be ignored. Rolston instead argues for the equivalent of a sacred covenant between human beings and the earth as a self-organizing corporate reality in its own right (218). Accordingly, beyond continued human well-being, the integrity of the earth as a corporate reality in its own right should be the ultimate unit of moral concern for human beings at this point in human history. "Earth is not something that we outgrow or rebuild and manage to our liking, it is the ground of our being.

We humans too belong on the planet; it is our home, as much as for all the others" (222).

At the end of his book, therefore, Holmes Rolston ends up with the same focus as Pope Francis in *Laudato si'*: care for our common home. Admittedly, Pope Francis addressed the issue of environmental change more from a pastoral than a scientific perspective, as with Rolston. But they both recognized the urgency of the issue and the need for an effective response from ordinary people as well as from civil and ecclesiastical authorities. In that sense they both implicitly endorse the thesis of Peter Berger and Thomas Luckmann in *The Social Construction of Reality*, namely, that human beings have over time collectively set in place the social systems that currently govern their lives; hence, that human beings can over time collectively change those systems as needed to improve the quality of their life together in society.[17]

Thereby, both Francis and Rolston, in my judgment, implicitly give preference to a systems-oriented approach to reality in which the deeper value of the individual entity is to be found in contributing to a socially constituted reality greater than itself. As Nancey Murphy and George F. R. Ellis propose in *On the Moral Nature of the Universe*, "Self-renunciation for the sake of the other is humankind's highest good."[18] I would only add that precisely in its advocacy of self-renunciation for the sake of a higher good has the church an unparalleled opportunity to lead rather than follow in altering the pattern of life in contemporary society for the better.

---

[17] Berger and Luckmann, *The Social Construction of Reality*, 49–50.

[18] Nancey Murphy and George F. R, Ellis, *On the Moral Nature of the Universe: Theology, Cosmology and Ethics* (Minneapolis: Fortress Press, 1996), 118.

Epilogue

My Intellectual Odyssey

I end with a brief historical review of how I came to write this book on a systems-oriented approach to church life. As a Jesuit seminarian in the 1950s and 1960s I learned quite well the philosophy and theology of Thomas Aquinas. So, when I was given permission for graduate studies in philosophy after ordination, I chose to study in Germany at the University of Freiburg in Breisgau and focus on another philosophical tradition, namely, German idealism, with particular attention to the middle and late philosophy of F. W. J. Schelling. My mentor, Eugen Fink (a colleague of Martin Heidegger at Freiburg), recommended that I commence my study of Schelling with his *Freiheitsschrift*, an analysis of the ongoing interplay of divine and human freedom within the workings of the cosmic process. At the very beginning of that book, Schelling notes the latent ambiguity in the German word *Grund* ("ground"), namely, that it could mean both "reason" or objective presupposition and "vital source" or principle of subjectivity. Schelling favored the latter interpretation and used it to explain how both divine and human freedom originated from a non-rational or feeling-oriented principle of existence and activity within one's subjectivity. When I first read this paragraph out of the *Freiheitsschrift*, I was completely taken aback. For it dawned on me in a flash that Schelling was setting forth an understanding of the Christian God-world relationship that was dramatically different from the understanding of the God-world relationship in Aquinas and the Scholastic tradition.

Aquinas and the classical metaphysical tradition attempted an objective, purely rational understanding of the God-world relationship in terms of divine primary and creaturely secondary causality. But human freedom of choice would seem to be vaguely expressed, if not ultimately lost, when it is explained in terms of top-down causal relations in which the creaturely secondary cause is the instrument of the divine primary cause in the execution of a preconceived plan.[1] Schelling, however, with his notion of *Grund* as vital source or principle of subjectivity, clearly allowed for the contingency of human free choice in that the individual's free choice could be for either good or evil. In a curious way, therefore, the human being is the primary cause of his or her own free decision. God is instead the secondary cause of that free decision, albeit an indispensable secondary cause in that God as Creator and Sustainer of the human being empowers the human being to make a free choice and to act upon it.[2]

A second major insight for the development of my own systems-oriented approach to reality also came to me during my student years at Freiburg. I had occasion to read Josiah Royce's book *The Problem of Christianity*, in which he proposes that communities exist in their own right even though they originate and are sustained in existence from moment to moment by a group of human beings who share a common

---

[1] Aquinas, *Summa theologiae* I, Q. 22, art. 2.

[2] Some neo-Thomists claim that God's primary causality vis-à-vis human beings is to empower them to make their own decisions. But then is God or the human being responsible for what happens as a result of a given decision? Especially if the decision is for something morally evil, is God still the primary cause of what happens? Or is the human being ultimately responsible for whatever happens (either for good or for evil)? If so, then God is, properly speaking, a secondary cause of that free decision since God only enables the human being to make a decision that is ultimately his or her own responsibility.

past and look forward to a common future.[3] Once again, I intuitively realized that, in following Royce on this point, I was departing from the Aristotelian/Thomistic metaphysics that I had learned in the seminary. Whereas Aristotle and Aquinas emphasized that the world is composed of individual entities (substances), Royce was implicitly claiming that communities represent a higher stage of existence and activity than the individual entities who are their constituent members.[4] Individual human beings, for example, are born into the community of a family, are conditioned by it in their early years, contribute to it in their adult years, and eventually die within the community of the extended, if not always the immediate, family. Human reality is, in other words, grounded in the ongoing existence of communities more than in the transient existence and activity of individual human beings who make up those communities from moment to moment.

The only problem with Royce's communitarian vision of physical reality is that it is too limited. For Royce, the physical world should be understood as a universal community of interpretation, with God or the Spirit as the chief Interpreter and all human beings as finite interpreters in various local communities of interpretation that over time will become integral members of this universal community.[5] What I was looking for, however, was a sense of community in which all entities, not just human beings and God, would be members of a universal community of interpretation and in their own way likewise interpreters within it.

The third and final preparatory insight for my systems-oriented understanding of the God-world relationship in this book came some years later when I began reading Whitehead's

---

[3] Josiah Royce, *The Problem of Christianity* (Chicago: University of Chicago Press, 1968), 229–49, esp. 248–49.

[4] Ibid., 80–81, 122.

[5] Ibid., 315–17, 318–19, 340, 383.

Process and Reality.[6] He stipulates that "the final real things of which the world is made up" are momentary self-constituting subjects of experience that in dynamic interrelation from moment to moment constitute a "society." Furthermore, the category of society applied to both living and living entities. Anything that endures over time and in most cases in space as well is a society, an ongoing unity-in-diversity of parts or members. Initially, I thought that I had found the perfect match for my own socially oriented worldview. To my great disappointment, however, I belatedly realized that Whitehead paid scant attention to the underlying ontological reality of societies as socially constituted entities that were more than and other than simply the collective unity of their constituent subjects of experience from moment to moment. By his own admission Whitehead was a philosophical atomist, someone who emphasized the ontological priority of individual entities over corporate realities like communities or institutions.[7] Admittedly, elsewhere in *Process and Reality* Whitehead claims that a society "is its own reason."[8] Likewise, in *Adventures of Ideas,* a book published after *Process and Reality,* he stipulates that "a society has an essential character, whereby it is the society that it is, and it also has accidental qualities which vary as circumstances alter."[9] Thus understood, a Whiteheadian society is much akin to an Aristotelian substance. But Whitehead fails to make clear their differences from one another in that passage.

I realized that I had to strike out on my own, and equivalently become a neo-Whiteheadian who adapts the master's scheme to suit his own goals and values. Initially I defined a Whiteheadian society as a structured field of activity for the dynamic interrelation of constituent actual entities from moment

---

[6] Alfred North Whitehead, *Process and Reality: An Essay in Cosmology,* corrected ed., ed. David Ray Griffin and Donald W. Sherburne (New York: Free Press, 1978).

[7] Ibid., 35.

[8] Ibid., 89.

[9] Alfred North Whitehead, *Adventures of Ideas* (New York: Free Press, 1967), 204.

to moment. For the term *field* is a common term within the physical sciences, above all, theoretical physics. Furthermore, most scientists claim that fields really exist in physical reality and thus are not simply mental constructs for organizing empirical data. Fields are empirically verifiable objective realities with definite properties that can be mathematically calculated. An electromagnetic field, for example, is a physical field produced by electrically charged objects, some of which are stable and others of which exhibit a flow or current. It made sense, accordingly, for me to claim that a Whiteheadian society is likewise a field, namely, an ongoing energy field that is structured by the dynamic interrelation of its constituent actual entities from moment to moment and yet exists in its own right and as a result sets boundaries or constraints on the dynamic interrelation of successive sets of constituent actual entities. The drawback to the use of the term *field* as a substitute for a Whiteheadian *society* was its oddness in terms of common-sense experience. It is hard, for example, to think of oneself as a structured field of activity for dynamically interrelated energy events (actual entities) taking place within it. Likewise, it is repugnant to common sense to claim that interpersonal relations between two human beings can be reduced to the ongoing exchange between the constituents of two dynamically interrelated energy fields.

Accordingly, in recent years I have instead worked with the notion of system, understood as an ongoing unity-in-diversity of constituent parts or members. A *system* is then (like the term *field*) an enduring objective reality that is more than simply the sum of its parts from moment to moment. For example, a mechanical system like an automobile does not completely collapse if an individual sparkplug or tire has to be replaced. Organisms and other life-systems, to be sure, are more dependent for their survival upon the functioning of key parts or members, for example, physical organs like the heart or lungs. But, if the constituent parts or members of all systems (living and nonliving) are momentary self-constituting subjects of experience (Whiteheadian actual entities), then logically all systems are metaphysically other than their constituent parts or members. For, a system is an inanimate thing, not a momentary subject of experience. It is the ongoing empirical byproduct or result of the dynamic interrelationship of momentary subjects of experience from moment to moment. Furthermore, the term *system* is commonly used by natural scientists in setting forth theories about the emergence of life from nonlife and eventually the emergence of rationality and self-consciousness from purely sentient self-awareness.

As a result, I felt encouraged to begin working on a systems-oriented approach to systematic theology, in particular, the explanation of some key Christian beliefs that have been historically hard to understand from a rational perspective. Instead of simply appealing to the mystery of the divine Being, I experimented with a systems-oriented approach to their explanation. For example, the doctrine of the Trinity makes unexpected good sense if the divine Persons are interpreted as three individual life-systems that co-constitute the corporate life-system of a divine Community. The doctrine of the incarnation likewise seems to be more readily intelligible if the divine and human natures in Jesus as the Word Incarnate are understood to be dynamically interrelated life-systems in which each maintains its own distinctive mode of operation, and yet both are involved in every thought, word, and action of Jesus. Sometimes, the divine Life-system in Jesus is clearly operative (for example, in performing miracles); other times the human life-system is more prominent (for example, when Jesus was tired or hungry, when he felt sad, and when he felt joyful). Thereby the traditional sharp division between the natural and the supernatural orders of being and activity in human life was transcended in the person of Jesus and by implication should likewise be transcended by all other human beings when acting under the influence of divine grace. Finally, the entire world of creation can then be seen in both natural and supernatural terms, namely, as a cosmic process that originated in a "Big Bang" or energy explosion from within the energy field proper to the divine Persons in their ongoing interpersonal relationship, is sustained in existence by ongoing contact with the three divine Persons, and will eventually be fully integrated, albeit in an altered state, into the trinitarian life of God at the end of the world.[10]

A Practical Test of
My Systems-Oriented Approach to Reality

Yet a good doctrinal understanding of the God-world relationship requires practical application to be truly effective. The methodology of "see-judge-act," initiated by Joseph Cardijn in dealing with the working classes in Belgium at the beginning of the twentieth century and then used so successfully by the bishops at Vatican II in composing *Gaudium et spes*,[11] prompted me to start thinking of a systems-oriented approach to practical church life, especially at the level of the local parish. For, as already noted many times in this book, systems-oriented thinking focuses on bottom-up organization, the energy found in the dynamic interrelation of constituent parts or members of the system from moment to moment, rather than on top-down organization coming from a fixed governing body.

In Chapter 4 on the nature of the church, accordingly, I applied a systems-oriented approach to the history of the church and its new status since Vatican II. For I wanted to make clear how the church has been historically governed by a top-down mode of operation from the very beginning of its existence. Yet events before, during, and after Vatican II gave promise of a new bottom-up approach to life in the church, above all, at the parish level. Edward Hahnenberg's relational approach to ministries in the administration of the local parish provided for me a strategy for implementing my bottom-up systems-oriented

---

[10] For a more detailed exposition of my argument for a systems-oriented trinitarian understanding of the God-world relationship, see Joseph A. Bracken, SJ, *The World in the Trinity: Open-Ended Systems in Science and Religion* (Minneapolis: Fortress Press, 2014).

[11] See Chapter 3 above.

approach to church life. All that was further needed was a concrete issue that went beyond a better organization of life at the parish level to have an impact on the broader reality of life in civil society. Fortunately, Pope Francis with his encyclical *Laudato si'* and Holmes Rolston with his systems-oriented approach to environmental ethics gave me the opening that I needed for a further practical application of my proposed systems-oriented approach to reality.

I end this book, then, with some sense of accomplishment in setting forth a new way to look at life both in the church and in civil society. Whether that sense of accomplishment will in the long run be justified is, of course, beyond my control. Other people, in the words of Joseph Cardijn, will have to see, judge, and act upon my proposal. But in any event I have concretely experienced what Pope Francis called "the joy of the gospel" in thus witnessing to others what I myself sincerely believe to be an appropriate remedy for some of the ills that adversely affect life in the contemporary church.

Index